Science and the God Elusion

A reflection on the conundrums of life

Robin Arthur

Foreword by Dr. Stephen Weppner
Professor of Physics, Eckerd College, Florida, USA

Cover Design: Aaron Arthur

Cover image: Helix Nebula, NGC 7293 or "The Eye of God". Copyright 2009 by ESO (European Southern Observatory) <eso.org> Reproduced under the Creative Commons Attribution 4.0 International License. The image size and colors have been altered from the original.

First printing: 2019

ISBN: 978-0-9730000-8-5

Published by Touch BASE
26, Forestside Crescent
Halifax, NS
B3M 1M4
Canada

To my grandchildren:
Liam and Elliot Cunningham, Nathaniel, Gabriel and Evangeline Arthur,
Edith and Agnes Selles

CHAPTERS

FOREWORD

This work by Robin Arthur is captivating: it's a book on the intersection of science and God, written from the perspective of a committed journalist and apologetic. This topic has often been overwrought with tired arguments either from frantic militant new-atheists who are mouthpieces at the altar of rationalism or academic theologians with a language so syntactical that the elation and wonder of the subject have been suppressed. What we have in front of us is a book of glorious mystery and deservedly the author uses windmills, frogs, love, joy, monkeys, poetry, grief and other subjects to animate the proceedings. This is as it should be since a discussion of science and God eventually centers on the limits of the empirical scientific worldview.

As the Nobel Prize winning physicist and pioneer of quantum mechanics, Erwin Schrödinger, noted: "Science is, very usually, branded as being atheistic. After what we said, this is not astonishing. If its world-picture does not even contain blue, yellow, bitter, sweet – beauty, delight, sorrow; if personality is cut out by agreement, how should it contain the most sublime idea that presents itself to the human mind?"[1] Indeed. Personality may be lacking in science but it is abundant in the pages that follow.

By way of introduction, I am a physicist at a liberal arts college, Eckerd, in Florida. I am active in research which involves the theory of smashing atoms together using the above-mentioned quantum mechanics, and I am a practicing Roman Catholic. I have co-taught for over fifteen years a course called 'A Culture of Science and Faith' with a Professor of Religious Studies who earned his degree from Princeton Theological Seminary. And yes, as a scientist, I agree with Arthur that science and religion are vibrant and worthy enterprises that should engage in dialogue to understand their similarities and differences in the search for truth.

Language and interpretation are important for this conversation. The new-atheists (the most popular are ostensibly called the four horsemen: Dawkins, Hitchens, Dennett, and Harris) want to reserve words for science's exclusive use: truth, reliable, rational, objective and exclusive; words for religion's use: faith, myth, sacred, dogma. Arthur sees these word games for what they are - games. Science and religion are human endeavors and thus both subjects have legitimate purposes for the words on both lists. The new-atheists want to build artificial barriers where none exist. The dogma of their rationalism solidifies the idea of God as the cruel, indifferent watchmaker and wizard. Arthur's interpretation of how Darwin's theory of evolution has been used by this motley crew in the cruelest terms to divide, is spot on. Why should the gene be selfish? Why is evolution a race of survival? Why is evolution conflated to the human endeavors of economics, theology, and class struggle? Arthur suggests that Darwin's theory should be interpreted as a call to unity and equal respect for all. Amen.

To attract an open-minded, perceptive individual in a dialogue on science and God there needs to be within a generous dose of humility and a receptiveness to encountering different opinions. I have a twenty-five-year history of reading both theology and science and the writings which stick are those which claim no definitive answers when none exist. Science's strength is centered on the act of disproving, not proving; of falsifying statements, not verifying them. This is a severe limitation but yet it also asserts that science is ultimately humble.

The title to this work implies that science cannot disprove God and it indicates another feature of science's limitations – that it is only in the business of disproving statements that describe how the empirical universe operates and nothing more. From this additional constraint should flow more humility and more reverence for mystery. Yet we see the practitioners of new atheism, both scientist and non-scientist, espouse a faith in the church of scientism, the belief that science is the only way to approach truth. As Arthur notes, new atheist scientists look at their spiritual scientific colleagues with bewilderment and insinuate mental lapses of contradictions or cognitive dissonance. They refuse to address the works of esteemed scientists who have written on religion: John Polkinghorne, Kenneth Miller, and Francis Collins. The writings of these theist scientists demonstrate objectively that they understand clearly the limitations of their science and have the requisite humility.

I contend that Arthur understands these scientific limitations seemingly better than new atheist scientists like Richard Dawkins, Jerry Coyne and Lawrence Krauss, who have been criticized repeatedly for their superficial understanding of scientific philosophy. One would think that practitioners of science should comprehend the limits of their profession, sadly this lesson in scientific humility is absent from most programs of science education and what replaces it for the new atheists is an arrogance which makes intellectual discussion near impossible. In deference to the intellectual atheists who understood / understand scientific limitations (like Friedrich Nietzsche, Bertrand Russell, and Peter Higgs), they have my respect. In contrast, to advance science to the preeminent human endeavor makes the new-atheists heirs to the enlightenment and logical positivism. Both movements failed by self-referencing contradictions (one cannot prove using logic, that logic is the only or best way towards truth – the theory of everything). Scientism has the same unfounded faith and it likewise fails tests of objectivity and intellectual rigor.

Ambiguity and nuance should also abound when discussing God. Thankfully it is at the heart of Heisenberg's Uncertainty Principle in physics, Gödel's Incompleteness Theorem in mathematics, and Arthur's work here. To accept this ambiguity and nuance it takes a child-like view, mirroring parables and other elements of the Hebrew Bible, the Christian Gospels, The Hindu Ramayana and Zen Buddhist Koans. New-atheists take this adherence to God as a willingness to never "grow up". Their straw-man Santa Claus, Easter-bunny, Flying Spaghetti Monsters miss the point entirely. Yes, believers do have traditions which involve realms of fantasy, supernatural, moral plays, paradoxes. They share much in common with Grimm Fairy Tales but also with Shakespeare's dramas, Western and Eastern Opera, heroic epics of all eras (Gilgamesh, Odyssey, The Lord of the Rings, etc.) Theism satisfies dimensions of the human heart, that tabulating the species of the Earth or the stars in the sky cannot approach. The beauty of music and our genuine need for it to release us from the mundane, speak volumes about the limitations of a singular-faceted world that contains only science as truth. All intelligent species are playful and imaginative through adulthood. Humans are especially receptive to this facet of life, a facet which has multiple layers of that ambiguity, wonder, and nuance (in reference to my Theology colleague's area of research). I enjoyed reading Arthur's book because it has not removed the playfulness, ambiguity, and joy from the discussion.

Another trademark of new-atheists is to criticize religion with either a purposefully immature or a lackadaisical approach to theology. As discussed earlier, this derives from their dogmatic belief in scientism. Their ill-conceived ego is so strong that they are emboldened to make pronouncements about the impracticality of studying theology, and about the uselessness of a deity in their worldview. They then feel validated to expound on fundamental questions of morality, evil, and human suffering. These issues are complex but they have been discussed by esteemed philosophers and theologians for thousands of years. The new atheist tackles these complex issues in a perverse, anti-intellectual way. Ignoring the past, in essence starting from scratch, they proclaim that religion is the cause of nearly all detriments. They use as their straw-men a theology of religious fundamentalism which they envelop in logical contradictions and a dogma which never evolves. As the sociologist Robert Bellah has explored, religion, like any human endeavor, does evolve as different generations and cultures understand differently, through revelation, the ultimate questions of our universe. Mystery has many layers, many sides, many nuances and thus can be approached in a multitude of ways.

To be only superficially challenged by the new-atheists with tags like *"God is not Great"* or the *"God Delusion"* or *"The Last Superstition"* plainly lays bare the bankruptcy of their understanding of modern Christian theology contained in the works of Hegel, Otto, Rahner, Tillich, Barth or Merton. I am frankly irked at these authors who think they can discuss philosophy and theology without confronting the scholars of the past. Arthur faces these foundational challenges with more objectivity than his new atheist counterparts. He discusses morality, grief, and evil as an intellectual who is aware and conversant with the past intellectuals from diverse spiritual foundations and he also combines it with a strong dose of his own personal narratives. His God is a personal God and thus I find this mix of intellect and emotion especially revelatory.

Is God relevant today is the question that Arthur approaches in the final chapter (and the appendix!). Here, as a conference organizer on spiritual diversity, he has brought together voices from different religions searching for commonality and meaning in this modern era. The similarities found in their message is revealing of the continuing evolution of religious thought. There is enough manna in these selections to know that religion in North America is vibrant and relevant and can lift anyone through a demanding week. In my lifetime there has been an increasing awareness of the need for interfaith dialogue to not only understand the other better, but to also reflect on one's own religious practices and re-evaluate what is foundational. It is also pertinent for religion to understand the radical elements which espouse violence against their own and others. These speakers, invited by the author, take on these challenges and are not afraid to ask hard questions of themselves and their audience. For theists, the best criticism comes from within. In these selections, are messages of perseverance, unity and joy. Again, a hearty Amen. That is because ultimately, we do not want voices that preach division and rancor, ones that divide people between the rational and the irrational to win the day. What we see in the following pages is a thoughtful blend of mythos and logos fostering wisdom, peace, and hope for those willing to listen. Okay, enjoy chasing windmills. Onward and upward...

Dr. Stephen Weppner
Professor of Physics,
Eckerd College,
Florida, USA

CHAPTER 1

Uncovering life's mystery is about chasing windmills

Tommy had just got back from the beach.
"Were there other children there?" asked his mother.
"Yes," said Tommy.
"Boys or girls?"
"How could I know! They didn't have any clothes on."
They see not what is there, but what they have been trained to see.[9]
Anthony de Mello, S.J. *The Heart of the Enlightened*

Charles Darwin's *Origin of Species* would have probably made a greater contribution to mankind if his theory of evolution taught man that because we probably come from a common ancestor, we are one family brought together by a distant blood connection. That perspective would have likely put an end to some of the greatest evils in our world – slavery, racial prejudice, nationhood and religious rivalry.

Instead, the theory appears to have stretched itself out to make a case for organisms evolving from elemental atoms and instructed by a self-creating universe of natural laws to suddenly flash into living tissues. That, in irreverent silence, was an attempt by a section of the scientific world to ignore the first cause argument - one that infers from causal logic, a self-creator or God as the cause of the universe.

But if life began in a primordial ocean with organisms evolving from elemental atoms and then instructed by a self-creating universe of natural laws, suddenly flashed into living tissues, why would human life be sacred at all? If then, any credence is to be given to this serendipity in an evolution theory that does not accept a first cause, why would we call the destruction of human life abominable?

It's just as well that Darwin, when making his observation that all living things have much in common, in their chemical composition, the cellular structure and their laws of growth and reproduction, admitted to inferring from that hypothesis that "all organic beings which have lived on this earth have descended from some primordial form into which life was first breathed."[1] In saying so, Darwin acknowledged the first cause.

That, of course, did not halt the scientific pursuit for an answer to how did the universe originate and how and when did life begin. That great debate about origins is as old as the hills.

Diagoras of Melos was a Greek poet of the 5th century BC who, at the time, was widely regarded as an atheist. He spoke out against Greek religion and the notion of gods and criticized the Eleusinian Mysteries – the secret religious rites of ancient Greece. The Athenians accused him of blasphemy and Diagoras reportedly went into hiding outside Athens and died in Corinth.[2]

Diagoras was a disciple of Democritus, an influential Ancient Greek, pre-Socratic philosopher essentially thought to be the first to formulate an atomic theory of the universe, and whose speculation on atoms bore a resemblance to the nineteenth century postulation of atomic structure. He was later regarded as being more of a scientist, rather than a Greek philosopher.[3]

Like Democritus, Epicurus (341-270 BC) taught that the universe is infinite, that all matter is made up of invisible particles, which today we know are atoms, and that we see evidence of the laws of nature as a result of atoms moving and interacting in empty space. He held the view that death marked the end of the body and of the soul thus dispensing with the notion of punishment in the afterlife.[4]

Then in the 15th and 16th centuries, it was the work of scientists like Copernicus – mathematician and astronomer, Galileo – now called the father of modern physics, and Newton who laid the groundwork for a keener understanding of the universe and possibly a secular notion of its mystery.

In the 17th and 18th centuries, the term 'rationalist' was often used to refer to free thinkers of an anti-clerical and anti-religious outlook, and for a time the word acquired a distinctly pejorative force.[5] Deism thus became influential in intellectual circles with Jacques Rousseau and Voltaire who declared: "If God does not exist, it would be necessary to invent him."

Deism takes the position that God exists as a first cause, that He is creator of the universe, but one that does not interfere directly with the created world or intervene in the affairs of humanity. Equivalently, deism can also be defined as the view which posits God's existence as the cause of all things – admits to the perfection seen in the order of the universe but rejects divine revelation or the direct intervention of God in the personal affairs of man.

Subsequently, in the nineteenth century, German atheist Karl Marx pushed the envelope further, pronouncing religion as an opiate of the people and Friedrich Nietzche coined the aphorism "God is dead." Atheism in the 20th century took a brutal course with the emergence of communist leaders Joseph Stalin, Mao Zedong and Pol Pot whose hostility to Christianity and Judaism and whose drive to repress and eliminate religion, saw heartless atrocities committed against their people, resulting in the deaths of hundreds of millions of their citizens.

At about the same time the advance of science brought new insights into the order of the universe and free thought, liberalism and deism progressed into what is now referred to as modern atheism. Albert Einstein defined the Creator essentially as the sum total of the physical laws which describe the universe, but proclaimed to be a Deist and did not regard the Creator as a personal God.

So, how influential is atheism today and how godless is the world? A new report by the Centre for the Study of Global Christianity at Gordon Conwell Theological Seminary in South Hamilton, Massachusetts, shows a decline worldwide with the number of atheists falling from 4.5 percent of the world's population in 1970 to two percent in 2010 and projected to drop to 1.8 percent by 2020.[6]

The progress of science may have riveted man's understanding of the universe and opened up a new curiosity about how we all came to be. But the exploration of science for an understanding of the origins of the universe and of life itself, has not as yet come anywhere close to unravelling the mysteries that surround man's most profound questions about why do we exist and where do we go from here?

Of course, science does not answer the question "Why?" So, let's work with the question "How?" Do we know, for example, how self-replicating organisms came about? How do the atoms of carbon or hydrogen floating in our heads, think up an algorithm? What caused life? Can we truly say we know?

Do scientists with secular convictions dodge these questions? In subsequent chapters, this book presents scientists who speak of a time when the ultimate theory will dawn and open a window on the mysteries of the universe, so that we might come to understand why we have a universe at all. That, they say, shall signal the triumph of human reason over all else. But human reason is finite and that fact demands a cautious and discerning approach to the mysterious.

British biologist and Oxford professor, Richard Dawkins, vigorously defends his argument that there almost certainly is no God, in his book *The God Delusion*.

Dawkins first came to prominence with his 1976 book *The Selfish Gene*, which popularised the gene-centred view of evolution. With his book *The Extended Phenotype* (1982), he introduced into evolutionary biology, the influential concept that the phenotypic effects of a gene are not necessarily limited to an organism's body, but can stretch far into the environment. Later, in *The Blind Watchmaker* (1986), he argues against the watchmaker analogy proposed by William Paley - an 18th century Christian apologist and philosopher - which posits that the complexity of living organisms

14

demands the existence of a Creator, just as the intelligent design of a clock would demand a watchmaker. Dawkins describes the evolution process comparable to a blind watchmaker – arguing that reproduction, mutation, and selection occur independent of a designer.[7]

Einstein stood aside from secular scientists, declaring that what separates him from that community of intellectuals is utter humility toward the mysteries of the universe. He has said that his response to the mysterious force that moves the constellations, has been one of awe. "My religiosity consists in a humble admiration of the infinitely superior spirit that reveals itself in the little that we, with our weak and transitory understanding, can comprehend of reality."[8]

Indeed, science can point the way, but as all agree, it can only cast a light on what it can see and not on what lies hidden from it. As yet a great deal lies out of the reach of science and frustratingly to the secular scientist, the absolute truths about the universe and of life's origins remain a bewildering mystery.

In the ongoing chapters, this narrative will seek to join the conversation and bring an understanding to the table about why the great masses of humanity are undeterred by scientific progress that is focused on breaking the God "mantra" and through a theory of everything pursuing the overthrow of the notion that God prevails.

CHAPTER 2

What science knows about the origin of the universe ...and of life

An enthusiastic young man who had just graduated
as a plumber was taken to see Niagara Falls.
He studied it for a minute, then said:
"I think I can fix this."[9]

Anthony de Mello, S.J. *Prayer of the Frog*

The book of Genesis in the Holy Bible opens with the lines: In the beginning, God created the heavens and the earth. The earth was without form, and darkness was on the face of the deep. And the spirit of God was hovering over the face of the waters. Then God said, "Let there be light," and there was light. *Genesis 1: 1-3.*

But the gospel according to science tells us that in the beginning was the Big Bang. It tells us that creation occurred at a single moment - about fourteen billion years ago - when a ball of powerful energy exploded. After the initial expansion, the universe cooled sufficiently to allow the formation of subatomic particles, and later simple atoms. Giant clouds of these primordial elements – mostly hydrogen and helium- later coalesced through gravity in halos of dark matter, eventually forming the stars and galaxies, the descendants of which are visible today.[1]

Up until the beginning of the twentieth century, most scientists presumed an infinite universe – a Steady State theory that adhered to the perfect cosmological principle that asserts the observable universe is basically the same at any time. Then American astronomer, Edwin Hubble`s findings in 1929 prompted cosmologists to conclude that the universe began at a single moment and scientists rejected the

16

Steady State model on the grounds that observational evidence points to a Big Bang cosmology with a finite age of the universe.[2]

Dr. Francis S. Collins is a physician-geneticist noted for his landmark discoveries of disease genes, and his administration of the Human Genome Project (HGP) whose goal was to map and understand the genes of human beings - the code of life. Commenting on Hubble's discovery he tells us in his book *The Language of God* that it actually led to the conclusion that the universe began at a single moment.

"Using the Doppler effect – the same principle that allows the state police to determine the speed of your car as you pass by their radar equipment, or that causes the whistle of an oncoming train to have a higher pitch than after it has passed you - Hubble found that everywhere he looked, the light in the galaxies suggested that they were receding from ours. The farther away they were, the faster the galaxies were receding. If everything in the universe is flying apart, reversing the arrow of time would predict that at some point all of these galaxies were together in one incredibly massive entity. Hubble's observations started a deluge of experimental measurements that over the last seventy years have led to the conclusion by the vast majority of physicists and cosmologists that the universe began at a single moment, commonly now referred to as the Big Bang. Calculations suggest it happened approximately 14 billion years ago"[3]

The Big Bang is now the accepted cosmological model for the universe. So, what we see is that creation happened all at once. Why, we do not know.

Scientists tell us that there is enough evidence behind the Big Bang theory. In 1964, US physicist Arno Penzias and radio-astronomer Robert Woodrow Wilson rediscovered the cosmic microwave background (CMB) estimating its temperature as 3.5K. The discovery of CMB radiation was important evidence for a hot early Universe as well as evidence against the rival Steady State theory.[4]

But, despite it all, even in the scientific world to this day, not everyone is convinced about how nature could have originated on its own. In the rat race for uncovering the mystery of creation, the scientific community appears to have hastened to ignore the first cause. So it's been convenient to postulate that ours is a self-creating universe. The Big Bang tells you that planets shot out of that ball of powerful energy, then after eons of time, temperatures on our planet cooled to form simple atoms and then chemicals floating across the universe randomly coalesced forming amino acids to create living organisms in a primordial ocean from which people like us were formed. The narrative forces the conclusion that the theory is ridden with serendipity and the observer therefore demands a metaphysical explanation to what sounds like a chain loop of miracles.

Rejection of the Big Bang

Sir Fred Hoyle, (June 1915 –August 2001) an English astronomer, who rejected the Big Bang theory had observed: "The notion that not only the biopolymer but the operating program of a living cell could be arrived at by chance in a primordial organic soup here on the Earth is evidently nonsense of a high order."[5] Though Hoyle declared himself an atheist, he was drawn to the conclusion that "a superintellect has monkeyed with physics, as well as with chemistry and biology, and that there are no blind forces worth speaking about in nature."[6] Hoyle's hypothesis, at least to me, provides some traction to the argument on origins– whether of life or the universe.

The desperate search for life's origin may have prompted some scientists to propose that life forms possibly appeared on this planet from outer space. The panspermia theory suggests that life on earth did not originate on our planet but was transported here from somewhere else in the universe.[7] Whatever be the case, while that second guess might tell us how life surfaced on earth, it does not tell us how life began.

How did life evolve?

The discovery in 1953 of the double helix, the twisted-ladder structure of deoxyribonucleic acid (DNA), by James Watson and Francis Crick marked a milestone in the history of science and gave rise to modern molecular biology, which is largely concerned with understanding how genes control the chemical processes within cells. In short order, their discovery yielded ground-breaking insights into the genetic code and protein synthesis.[8] While that research was truly remarkable, critics say that does not provide convincing evidence that we are evolved pond scum. So how did life evolve? Is life inevitable?

It is very natural to respond with some perplexity to this complex proposition of a self-creating universe. The probability of obtaining even a single functioning protein by chance combination of amino acids, a hypothesis Hoyle had scoffed at, is what makes acceptance of theories of the origin of life dubious. Will the passage of time, change the perspective? Let's see.

Stephen Weppner, Professor of Physics at Eckerd College, Florida, tells me it is well known that science, like religion, is a paradigm, so a theist should not worry at any moment about science challenging faith. "And if science is only a paradigm that can change, it thus screams its limited ability to observe truth," he says. "There is no disagreement about the fact that religion can be couched in the same language. But science is not special. It is one more human endeavor that is open to the same limitations and faults as any other human endeavor, including religion."

Dr. Weppner also tells me that fifty years ago the argument was that scientists will never explain why flowers bloom because it is the purview of God. "But scientists found out how flowers bloom sixteen years ago. Likewise, someday science may put amino acids together to form a complex molecule. That should not diminish God. Like evolution itself, man's understanding of God's creation is a work in progress."

Indeed, science has told us what it knows from what it has seen. But the truth may be elusive because science cannot tell us with empirical evidence what it cannot see. So the answers to the profound questions man has posed – the questions about why do we have a universe instead of nothing at all; or why am I here; or what happens after death – lie behind a closed door. Science is silent on that.

CHAPTER 3

Darwin's revolutionary idea of evolution

Charles Darwin, (1809-1882), an English naturalist, biologist and theologian, was swayed by the argument advanced by William Paley, the moral philosopher whose parable - of stumbling on a watch on the moor and deducing by its design, the existence of a watchmaker – resonated with many people in the nineteenth century. It continues to be a parable often repeated by many people today: Life with its complexity appears designed, so there must be a designer....a Creator.

This was Paley's watchmaker analogy: "In crossing a heath, suppose I pitched my foot against a stone and were asked how the stone came to be there; I might possibly answer that, for anything I knew to the contrary, it had lain there forever. Nor would it perhaps be easy to show the absurdity of this answer. But suppose I had found a watch upon the ground and it should be inquired how the watch happened to be in that place; I should hardly think of the answer, which I had before given, that for anything I knew, the watch might have always been there. The watch must have had a maker: that there must have existed, at some time, and at some place or other, an artificer or artificers, who formed it for the purpose which we find it actually to answer; who comprehended its construction and designed its use. Every indication of contrivance, every manifestation of design, which existed in the watch, exists in the works of nature, with the difference, on the side of nature, of being greater or more, and that in a degree which exceeds all computation."[1]

Like Paley, Darwin too, saw design in nature as proof of a Creator. But upon examining the diverse species of life forms and the fossilized remains of primordial organisms on the Galapagos islands in South America, he had a change of heart. Then in 1859, he finally wrote and published his theory in *The Origin of Species,* postulating that all species of life or groups of organisms have descended, over time, from common ancestors. His proposition that all species of life have descended over time from common ancestors is now widely accepted in the scientific world and beyond.

Darwin set out his theory of evolution by natural selection as an explanation for adaptation and speciation and defined natural selection as the principle by which each slight variation of a trait, if useful, is preserved. In *Origin* this is what he writes: "Owing to this struggle for life, any variation, however slight and from whatever cause proceeding, if it be in any degree profitable to an individual of any species, in its infinitely complex relations to other organic beings and to external nature, will tend to the preservation of that individual, and will generally be inherited by its offspring. The offspring, also, will thus have a better chance of surviving, for, of the many individuals of any species which are periodically born, but a small number can survive. I have called this principle, by which each slight variation, if useful, is preserved, by the term of Natural Selection, in order to mark its relation to man's power of selection."[2]

Darwin's ideas were inspired by the observations that he had made on the second voyage of HMS Beagle (1831–1836), and by the work of the political economist, Thomas Robert Malthus, who, in *An Essay on the Principle of Population* (1798), discussed the importance of checking population growth to keep it in tandem with food production capacity. The Malthusian theory that developed, asserted that population growth occurs exponentially and that if not checked, food supply would not catch up, thus resulting in a struggle for existence. The theory resonated with Darwin and inspired by Malthus's idea of the struggle for existence, he set out to propose his view of adaptation.

Darwin wrote: "If during the long course of ages and under varying conditions of life, organic beings vary at all in the several parts of their organisation, and I think this cannot be disputed; if there be, owing to the high geometrical powers of increase of each species, at some age, season, or year, a severe struggle for life, and this certainly cannot be disputed; then, considering the infinite complexity of the relations of all organic beings to each other and to their conditions of existence, causing an infinite diversity in structure, constitution, and habits, to be advantageous to them, I think it would be a most extraordinary fact if no variation ever had occurred useful to each being's own welfare, in the same way as so many variations have occurred useful to man. But if variations useful to any organic being do occur, assuredly individuals thus characterised will have the best chance of being preserved in the struggle for life; and from the strong principle of inheritance they will tend to produce offspring similarly characterised. This principle of preservation, I have called, for the sake of brevity, Natural Selection. It leads to the improvement of each creature in relation to its organic and inorganic conditions of life; and consequently, in most cases, to what must be regarded as an advance in organisation."[3]

Natural selection is now one of the cornerstones of modern biology. That being said, the curious question lingers: How convincing is Darwin's theory as an argument on the origins of life? In his chapter on Instinct, Darwin refers to three most wonderful of all known instincts. He points to the instinct which leads the cuckoo to lay her eggs in other birds' nests; the slavish instincts of certain ants; and the comb-making power of the hive-bee to demonstrate how instincts in a state of nature have become modified by selection. But he also slips in a line of caution on instinct: "I must premise, that I have nothing to do with the origin of the primary mental powers, any more than I have with that of life itself. We are concerned only with the diversities of instinct and of the other mental qualities of animals within the same class."[4] In short, Darwin steers away from the conversation about the origin of life itself.

In an upcoming chapter in this book, the point is made that the Church does not have to stand in opposition to science on the hypothesis it has so far produced to advance one's understanding of how life began. Evolution may well have been a divine piece of work.

Theists have, for example, argued the fact that if genuinely irreducible complexity could be properly demonstrated, it would wreck Darwin's theory. The complexity of the eye, is one of them. Darwin initially confessed that it was "absurd" to posit that the human eye evolved through spontaneous mutation and natural selection. But later on he went on to argue that by reason he was drawn to the conclusion that the difficulty of believing that a perfect and complex eye could be formed by natural selection, can hardly be considered real.

He wrote: "To suppose that the eye, with all its inimitable contrivances for adjusting the focus to different distances, for admitting different amounts of light, and for the correction of spherical and chromatic aberration, could have been formed by natural selection, seems, I freely confess, absurd in the highest possible degree. Yet reason tells me, that if numerous gradations from a perfect and complex eye to one very imperfect and simple, each grade being useful to its possessor, can be shown to exist; if further, the eye does vary ever so slightly, and the variations be inherited, which is certainly the case; and if any variation or modification in the organ be ever useful to an animal under changing conditions of life, then the difficulty of believing that a perfect and complex eye could be formed by natural selection, though insuperable by our imagination, can hardly be considered real."[5]

In another passage in *Origin*, Darwin distances himself from any conversation that proposes a self-creating universe where life cells develop from non-living matter and, in fact, alludes to a Creator breathing life into primordial forms.

He wrote: "Analogy would lead me one step further, namely, to the belief that all animals and plants have descended from some one prototype. But analogy may be a deceitful guide. Nevertheless, all living things have much in common, in their chemical composition, their germinal vesicles, their cellular structure, and their laws of growth and reproduction. We see this even in so trifling a circumstance as that the same poison often similarly affects plants and animals; or that the poison secreted by the gall-fly produces monstrous growths on the wild rose or oak-tree. Therefore I should infer from analogy that probably all the organic beings which have ever lived on this earth have descended from some one primordial form, into which life was first breathed."[6]

The explanatory note to "breathed" in a subsequent edition of the book suggests that Darwin does not discuss origins. Instead, he invokes the Creator –and that image is reflected in the book's final paragraph. This is the text in the first edition of *Origins*:

"There is grandeur in this view of life, with its several powers, having been originally breathed[*] into a few forms or into one; and that, whilst this planet has gone cycling on according to the fixed law of gravity, from so simple a beginning, endless forms most beautiful and most wonderful have been and are being evolved."[7] In the subsequent edition, Darwin enters the phrase *by the Creator* to follow the word *"breathed."*

But go back to Darwin's piquant observation that "there is grandeur in this view of life..." In that narrative, he contemplates on the plants of many kinds, with birds singing on the bushes, with various insects flitting about, and with worms crawling through the damp earth, and invites the reader to reflect on the fact that these elaborately constructed forms, so different from each other in so complex a manner, have all been produced by laws acting around us.

Indeed, there is grandeur in that view of life. But then, science greats of the class of Albert Einstein and Carl Sagan have always affirmed the awesome perfection that is seen in the order of the universe or the laws of nature and Einstein openly declared his belief in an abstract and impersonal Supreme Being inspired by the sight of the constellations.

If then, the order in the universe can be attributed to a first cause, why cannot the laws of nature, according to Darwin, "acting around us" and working for the preservation of favoured races in the struggle for life, be attributed to the same lawgiver. Darwin thought it important to reference the Creator when he spoke of organic beings descending from some primordial form "into which life was first breathed". Why then does a minuscule intelligentsia of our global society not come to terms with this truth?

The controversy over the finer points of Darwin's evolution theory comes not singularly from religionists, but according to reports, from credible scientific dissent as well. But this book does not seek to go there. The point this chapter makes is that Darwin's theory does not appear to be concerned with ultimate origins, despite its name, and that neither does he seem to explain absolute beginnings. In *Origin*, he merely opens up a new window on the mutation of species and explains why he sees the evolution process progress through natural selection and not by independent divine fiat.

He has admitted to feeling compelled to look to a first cause with an intelligent mind in some degree analogous to that of man and in so doing gently admitted to an appreciation of the grandeur of life with its several powers, having been originally breathed by the Creator into a few forms or into one.

Of course, Darwin's stance on whether or not this universe has a Creator, shifted with time. He is reported to have said at one time: "Agnostic would be the most correct description of my state of mind." But at another time this is what he has said: "Another source of conviction in the existence of God, connected with the reason and not with the feelings, impresses me as having much more weight. This follows from the extreme difficulty or rather impossibility of conceiving this immense and wonderful universe, including man with his capacity of looking far backwards and far into futurity, as the result of blind chance or necessity. When thus reflecting I feel compelled to look to a first cause having an intelligent mind in some degree analogous to that of man; and I deserve to be called a Theist."[8]

So, what does the *Origin of Species* mean to man? Of course, to the secularist, it would mean we have evolved from apes and that God was not involved in the evolution of species. But what it does not mean to anyone, who keenly senses Darwin's cautionary tone, is that life came about independently from primordial matter.

The progress of science since Darwin's day has, very apparently, been monumental and biologists today say that they can see the variation Darwin postulated is supported by naturally occurring mutations in DNA. Darwin's theory of natural selection provides a fundamental framework for understanding the relationship of all living things. It does not, however, provide a convincing argument about the origins of man and the complexities of his intellect and metaphysical nature, evolving through the mutability of species.

So, in his riposte to Professor Dawkins' book, *The God Delusion*, John Cornwell writes in his book *Darwin's Angel*: "Well, there's a lot to be said for Charles Darwin's theory of natural selection as an explanation for the origin of species. But only a double-eyed fundamentalist Darwinian would deny that an evolutionary perspective furnishes no more than a slender contribution to what drives human behaviour, especially in the cultural sphere of the imaginative, the poetic, the artistic."[9]

Cornwell's observation defends the argument that the complexity of man's intellect and his metaphysical nature cannot be convincingly explained citing the genetic process within natural selection.

CHAPTER 4

The scientific and spiritual are a twain that can meet

The recent polls suggest that believers reject evolution because it appears to contradict some sacred texts which describe God's role in creation. In Christianity and Judaism, the great creation story of Genesis 1 and 2 is a solid bedrock of truth for billions of believers. "In the beginning, God created the heavens and the earth." Then the subsequent lines describe the creation of light, waters, the firmament, land and vegetation, the sun, moon and stars, fish and birds and then living creatures and finally man and woman.

In a presentation at the third Spiritual Diversity Conference held in Halifax in 2016, Syed Moustaffa al-Qazwini, President of the Shia Muslim Council of Southern California told delegates, the Quran states: "Humankind, we have created you from a single cell of male and female and made you into tribes so you may recognize one another."

But sacred texts do not pitch the Catholic church or religious institutions in opposition to science. The Church's opposition to Gallileo's postulation of a heliocentric solar system in the early seventeenth century, of course, was an embarrassment. But that cannot take away the truth that the Catholic church has also been key to the development of science. The physicist who first proposed the "Big Bang" theory in 1927 was George Lemaitre, a Catholic priest. Lemaitre was an astronomer and professor of physics at the Catholic University of Leuven. Nicolas Steno, a 17th century bishop, helped establish modern geology and paleontology. Gregor Mendel, a 19th century Augustian Friar, is the father of modern genetics.[1]

This chapter, precisely therefore, seeks to define the points at which the scientific and the spiritual can meet because there exists strong dependencies between the two. It's just as well that the great sage of the Church, Saint Augustine of Hippo, had called for caution in the way biblical texts are interpreted.

He wrote, with specific reference to Genesis: "In matters that are so obscure and far beyond our vision, we find in Holy Scripture, passages which can be interpreted in very different ways without prejudice to the faith we have received. In such cases, we should not rush in headlong and so firmly take our stand on one side, that, if further progress in the search for truth justly undermines this position, we too fall with it."[2]

The scientific deduction is that the Big Bang occurred approximately 14 billion years ago and that affirmation is a radical departure from the Genesis story of the six-day creation. That scientific contention had obviously outraged great masses of the world's Christian population and in October 2014 Pope Francis intervened to sound a note of calm and reportedly told audiences at the Vatican that "God is not a magician with a magic wand" and that the theory of evolution and the big bang does not in any way contradict the Genesis story.

Apparently, at the heart of this great misunderstanding between the scientific and the spiritual concept of time is etymology. As theologians explain, the six-day creation story must be accepted from the etymological foundations of the Hebrew language through which conduit Genesis was first inspired. The Hebrew word for "day" seen in Genesis, is yôm. But yôm relates to the concept of time. The word 'day' is used in somewhat the same way as in the English language, examples: "In my grandfather's day," or "In the day of the dinosaurs..." Thus "yom," in its context, is sometimes translated as *time* (Gen 4:3, Is. 30:8); *year* (I Kings 1:1, 2 Chronicles 21:19, Amos 4:4); *age* (Gen 18:11; Joshua 23:1), *season,* (Genesis 40:4, Joshua 24:7); *epoch* or *24-hour day* (Genesis 1:5)[3]

Saint Augustine, referred to as Doctor of the Church, repeatedly harked back to the meaning of time in his books *The Literal Meaning of Genesis*, the *Confessions* and *The City of God* and proposed that

God is outside of time. In 2 Peter 3:8 the line is emphatic: *"With the Lord, a day is like a thousand years and a thousand years are like a day."*

Those who interpret Genesis in absolutely literal terms conclude that the earth is only 5,000 years old and therefore reject the scientific view of the age of the universe. But the modern religious believer thinks otherwise. That is because it is fair to take the view that God would have been the author of evolution and the author of the Big Bang. In taking that position you see that neither the Big Bang nor evolution in nature contradict the creation story. Indeed, if this was the way the Creator chose to structure the universe, so be it.

On 26 June of the new millennium, news of a scientific breakthrough brought the scientific and spiritual worlds together. That summer morning, Dr. Collins, the director of the International Human Genome Project and Craig Venter, the president of Celera Corporation, stood shoulder to shoulder with US President Bill Clinton in the East Room of the White House to celebrate the completion of the first survey of the Entire Human Genome.

In his speech Clinton compared this human sequence map to the one that Meriwether Lewis had presented President Thomas Jefferson in that very room a little over two hundred years ago. The map by Lewis was the product of his courageous expedition across the American frontier, all the way to the Pacific. But then, President Clinton jumped from the scientific to the spiritual realm:

"Today's announcement represents more than just an epic-making triumph of science and reason" he said. "After all, when Galileo discovered he could use the tools of mathematics and mechanics to understand the motion of celestial bodies, he felt, in the words of one imminent researcher, that he had learned the language in which God created the universe. Today we are learning the language in which God created life. We are gaining ever more awe for the complexity, the beauty, the wonder of God's most divine and sacred gift. With this profound new knowledge, humankind is on the verge of gaining immense, new power to heal."[4]

The narrative confirms that there can be a meeting point between the scientific and spiritual world views.

There is no denying that science is the only empirical way to understand the natural world and comprehend some of those essential truths about the universe. But critical to man's search for truth that surrounds us is the question about how we got here, why at all, and where are we headed? Science is silent on that. So it really would make sense to seek those answers in the spiritual and mystical realms. In taking both those paths along the journey of understanding we might achieve a synthesis of perception and bring together the spiritual and scientific world views to lay the foundations for a bedrock of truth.

If religion dwells in the realm of human consciousness to seek life's purpose, it is desirable as history has proved, that it shies away from the twain in which science seeks its truth driven by what is empirically evidenced. But as observed earlier in this chapter - the Catholic church has been key to the development of science – in the fields of astronomy, physics, paleontology and genetics. What this says is that science and spirituality can work together as most scientists even in the twenty first century will testify to. That is because scientists like people in other disciplines or streams of study are also driven by the aspiration to seek the truth in realms where science has not tread. The conundrums of life challenge all of us and a harnessing of the scientific and spiritual paradigms may be the best way of lighting the way ahead.

Einstein stated it quite plainly: "The situation may be expressed by an image: science without religion is lame, religion without science is blind."[5]

CHAPTER 5
The mysteries of the universe that science cannot unravel

A guru promised a scholar a revelation of greater consequence than anything contained in the scriptures. When the scholar eagerly asked for it, the guru said:

"Go out into the rain and raise your head and arms heavenward.

That will bring you the first revelation."

The next day the scholar came to report: "I followed your advice and water flowed down my neck – and I felt like a perfect fool."

"Well," said the guru "for the first day that's quite a revelation, isn't it?"[9]

Anthony de Mello, S.J. *Prayer of the Frog*

The world-renowned physicist, the late Dr. Stephen Hawking in a 2010 interview on the *Larry King Live* show said something that may be challenged: "God may exist, but science can explain the universe without the need for a Creator."[1] Is that really true?

Karlo Broussard, a Catholic apologist, notes that since science relies on the inductive method (to validate its hypothesis), it follows that scientists can never be absolutely certain that their theories explaining the universe are complete. "My mentor and friend, Fr. Robert J. Spitzer likes to say, 'Science cannot know what it has not yet discovered, because it has not yet discovered it.'" In other words, the argument is that scientists can be certain only about what they have *already* discovered through empirical observation.

"Certainty can never be had for whether there is some piece of data enshrouded in the past or a piece of data yet to be encountered that shifts the paradigm. Therefore, there necessarily exists in science, a perpetual openness to discovering something new that could alter its current theory about the universe." He concludes saying: "So, the claim that God doesn't matter because science can sufficiently explain the universe is unfounded."[2]

As this chapter unfolds, what will become increasingly clear is that so many mysteries of the universe are yet beyond the grasp of science or scientists and theories of all kinds are being revisited. The Big Bang is only one of them.

In a new book *Know This*, edited by John Brockman, Paul J. Steinhardt, Theoretical Physicist and Director, Princeton Center for Theoretical Science contends, "The Big Bang cannot be what we thought it was"[3]

Rudy Brucker, mathematician and computer scientist, affirms in the same book, that many cosmologists now think our spatial universe is infinite. "Thirty years ago, it was widely believed that our spatial universe is the finite 3D hypersurface of a 4D hypersphere – analogous to the finite 2D surface of a 3D sphere." In his conclusion, he writes: "Well as far as I can see, we're living in one of those times when cosmologists have no clear idea of what's going on. They don't understand the start of the cosmos, nor cosmic inflation, nor dark energy, nor dark matter. You might say they don't know jack."[4]

The other elusive pursuit, in the scientific community, is the search for the origins of life.

In 1924, Alexander Oparin, a Russian biochemist, put forward a hypothesis suggesting that life on Earth developed through a gradual chemical evolution of carbon-based molecules in the Earth's primordial soup. That was about the time the British biologist J. B. S. Haldane was independently proposing a similar theory. Oparin suggested that different types of coacervates - viscous liquids - could have formed in the Earth's primordial ocean and been subject to a selection process that led, eventually, to life. But while Oparin himself was unable to conduct experiments to test any of these ideas, later researchers tried.[5]

So, in 1953, biochemist Stanley Miller attempted an experiment to investigate whether chemical self-organization could have been possible in a primordial ocean. While there was initial euphoria over the results, subsequent experiments failed to extend those findings.

Now this is what Dr. Gerald Schroeder has to say about Miller's experiment in his book *The Hidden Face of God*: "We can predict all the elements used in life, but there is no indication that we can predict amino acids joining together in chains of hundreds of thousands of units to form proteins and then proteins combining into the symbiotic relationships we refer to as life. When in 1953, Stanley Miller, then a graduate student at The University of Chicago, produced a few amino acids through purely random reactions among chemicals found naturally throughout the universe, the scientific community felt the problem of life's origin had been solved. Far from it. Subsequent experiments failed to extend his results. Thermodynamics favours disorder over order. Attempting to get those amino acids to join into any sort of complex molecules has been one long study in failure. The emergence of the specialized complexity of life, even in its most simplest forms, remains a bewildering mystery."[6]

Likewise, we know that several other questions beg an answer. Science tells us that all of us have previously inert atoms – whether carbon, hydrogen or oxygen - floating in our heads. How have these atoms suddenly flashed into intelligent life? I believe that to man and the scientist this remains a niggling mystery. All of this, at best, demonstrates the point that science has to discover a whole lot more to make that confident assertion that it can explain the universe without God.

In his book *The God Delusion*, Professor Dawkins raises the question about the six fundamental physical constants which are believed to hold all around the universe – those six numbers finely tuned in a way that if they were slightly different, the universe would probably be unfriendly to life. How those fundamental physical constants were so finely tuned so as to make the universe hospitable to life is still a mystery. So how does one respond to this?

Dr. Weppner's observation on the matter is that there is the strong and weak anthropic principle. "Dawkin's argument relies heavily on the weak version which only states that to ask this question there must be intelligent life, thus it is really not too important. To give any strength to this argument the scientist is probably a proponent of the 'multiverse theory' which has gained traction in the last 25 years. If this was *the only* universe, then it would be remarkable but if there are *countless* universes (created out of nothing) then we are a "special one" which allows life to exist and because we are here we ask this question. Note that the multiverse theory is not really a scientific theory since it would be really hard to find empirical evidence of another universe (our scientific laws only hold for *this* universe). Now maybe in 500 years we could create a universe in a beaker then that would be indirect evidence."

Furthermore, Dr. Weppner notes that the strong anthropic principle hints towards a creator because it is the "wizard with dials" theory. "It assumes universes are only products of a Creator (finite or infinite). One weakness, in general, of the anthropic principle is that it is not really creative. There are probably infinite ways to create life. We are in a box, we think our box is very special, but how do we know how special or unique since we do not have the brain capacity to envision other special boxes. Are you familiar with 'A Puddlian Fable' by Feinberg and Shapiro? It details this species that grows up in this wonderful puddle, thinking that it is 'perfect for life' however unaware, beyond the next rock lives a human civilization."

When Hawking first articulated his ideas about the 'Theory of Everything' in his 1988 book: *A Brief History of Time,* he wrote: "If we do discover a complete theory [of physics], it should in time be understandable in broad principle by everyone. Then we shall all, philosophers, scientists and just ordinary people, be able to take part in the discussion of why it is that we and the universe exist. If we find the answer to that, it would be the ultimate triumph of human reason—for then we would truly know the mind of God."[7]

But as Cornwell points out in his book *Darwin's Angel*, in 2004, "Stephen Hawking, finally came around to the conclusion that the pursuit of the theory of everything was in vain. His decision was a result of revisiting a proof that has fascinated mathematical physicists for many decades."[8] The dream of a final theory is apparently utopic.

A solid cadre of the scientific community has, down the ages, despaired of the fact that man's comprehension of the universe is limiting and the fact, as well, that any insights into the origins of life are, at this time, only a hypothesis.

So how do we draw any comfort from this despair? I propose, that comes from acknowledging with venerable humility that there is something greater than ourselves. Man must stand in awe at the sight of the universe, at the miracle of life, because we see the grandeur but only dimly understand how it all comes together.

CHAPTER 6

The God that eludes science - the mystery deepens

All the philosophers, divines and doctors of the law were assembled in court for the trial of Mullah Nasruddin. The accusation was a serious one: he had been going from town to town saying: "Your so-called religious leaders are ignorant and confused." So he was charged with heresy, the penalty for which was death.

"You may speak first," said the Caliph. The Mullah was perfectly self-possessed. "Have paper and pens been brought in," he said. "Give them to the ten wisest men in this august assembly."

To Mullah Nasruddin's amusement, a great squabble broke out among the holy men as to who was the wisest among them. When the contention died down and each of the chosen ten was equipped with paper and pen, the Mullah said: "Have each of them write down the answer to the following question: WHAT IS MATTER MADE OF?"

The answers were written down and handed to the Caliph who read them out. One said: It is made of "nothing." Another said, "Molecules".

Yet another "Energy." Others: "Light", ``Metaphysical Being'' and so on.

Then said Nasruddin to the Caliph:

"When they come to an agreement on what matter is, they will be fit to judge questions of the spirit. Is it not strange that they cannot agree on something that they themselves are made of, yet they are unanimous in their verdict that I am a heretic."[12]

Anthony de Mello, S.J. *Prayer of the Frog*

"My faith is founded on reason," I told Isaac in a conversation not long ago.

"How do you mean?" he quipped: "Are you saying that like the apostle Thomas, you shall believe only when you have put your hand in His side?"

Isaac, who is my sister Belinda's husband, was referencing the gospel story of the apostle who refused to believe Jesus Christ had risen from the tomb, days after his crucifixion and had met with his fellow disciples in the Upper Room, also known as the Cenacle in the Old City of Jerusalem on Mount Zion. "Until I put my hand in His side, I shall not believe," the apostle Thomas had said. In the flash of a moment, I realized my utterance lacked clarity. Of course, I would like to think that my belief is founded on reason. But faith is something else. So I quickly responded: "No. That's not it. If that is what I meant, I would be talking 'science'. But what I am really saying is that my faith is founded on the fact that the Christ has put His hand in my side and which is why I believe. Now that's mysticism."

It's no great second guess that the masses of humanity on the planet, have likewise, felt the mystical touch of the Creator in many wondrous ways: even if it be in the brilliant sunset, the unfolding of a miracle, in the strains of a musical cantata.

Kurt Vonnegut, an agnostic and one of America's great writers says this in his book *A Man Without a Country:* "If I should ever die, God forbid, let this be my epitaph: The only proof he needed for the existence of God was music".[1]

But Professor Dawkins dismisses a similar allusion to music, in another context. "Beethoven's late quartets are sublime. So are Shakespeare's sonnets. They are sublime if God is there and they are sublime if he isn't. They do not prove the existence of God; they prove the existence of Beethoven and of Shakespeare."[2]

That this observation should be made by so brilliant a scientist as Professor Dawkins underpins the fact that mysticism is ineffable, as the 19th century scientist and mystic William James posits later in this chapter.

So what is mysticism? It's about connecting with the God you cannot see. It's about recognising this mysterious fact, like do the masses of humanity across different faiths on the planet; that you do not turn to physics and mathematics to see the face of God when all anyone can do to see that face is to open one's eyes and see His goodness pass you by.

In an Old Testament passage (Exodus 33: 20-23) God says to Moses "I will do the very thing you have asked, because I am pleased with you and I know you by name." Then Moses said, "Now show me your glory." And the Lord said, "I will cause all my goodness to pass in front of you, and I will proclaim my name, the Lord, in your presence. I will have mercy on whom I will have mercy, and I will have compassion on whom I will have compassion. But you cannot see my face, for no one may see me and live."

Cornwell, in his riposte to Dawkins' book *The God Delusion* writes: "At the outset of your book, you insist that religion must be scientifically or empirically verifiable. And yet for most of those who have studied religion down the ages, it is as much a product of the imagination as art, poetry and music."[3]

It would be nice to consider the fact that love is a very real thing, too. But it cannot be empirically verifiable. You cannot deny its pervading spirit and yet you cannot investigate the chemistry of love in a laboratory of science. So while you may never discover through science alone, evidence of the existence of a God, you can marvel at His wondrous work in the birth of a child, the colours of the rainbow, the breaking dawn.

Perhaps you have stopped to wonder why the sunflower follows the sun through a twenty-four-hour cycle – turning east to greet the sun in the morning and later turning west at dusk. Then have you stopped to wonder why they stop tracking the sun upon reaching maturity? Science might explain that as being the plant's response to sunlight in the growth phase. But that does not take away the wonder of creation present in the many things that surround us.

Have you looked out of the window while on a flight to anywhere? Did you look down upon the masses of humanity as the plane cruised at a height of so many thousand feet, scaled the hills and penetrated through the clouds and consider how insignificant we must be for anyone watching from above? Did the overwhelming awe that filled your spirit come from knowing there's something greater than yourself? The humility of the human spirit to recognize that, lets you sense the touch of this grandeur.

In moments like these, the mystic inside you opens your soul to the awesome wonder of the lofty mountains, the peaceful serenity of the valley, the burst of the waves, the rolling thunder, the bloom of the rose, the birthing of a newborn, the instinct of the mother, or compassion of the altruistic.

In one of his notes to me that outlined his view of the mystical, Reverend Father Owen Connolly, a priest who serves at the Archdiocese of Halifax, Canada, referred to an ancient mystical tradition in many of the faiths including Christianity, that suggests that we are given three eyes with which to look at life. First, we have the eye of the flesh serving input such as sight; second, the eye of reason and reflection; third, the eye of mystical gaze which builds on the first two eyes, namely the eye of the heart.

Then with a reference to Thomas Merton, the great Trappist Monk of the Abbey of Gethsemani, Kentucky in the 1950s, who reintroduced Christians to contemplative prayer which lay dormant since the sixteenth century, Connolly talked of how mystical prayer can lead man to look at life in these dangerous times, from the eye of the heart.

Fr. Karl Rahner, a German Jesuit and one of the most influential theologians in the twentieth century, in Roman Catholic tradition, said sometime before his death: "The only Christians who will survive in the post-modern world, will be those who are mystics." Connolly, presenting the Jesuit's observation at the 2016 Interfaith conference I had hosted in Halifax, told delegates: "At the time, I don't think the statement resonated with the Catholic world, in the same way as it does today, for as time goes on and we go deeper and deeper into the 21st century, many are beginning to realize just how important this insight should be for us. Why is it so challenging for Westerners?"

Connolly was making the point that it is so challenging because we are so uncomfortable with the whole notion of mystery. "We are cerebral people, in many ways dualistic and so if we are not able to explain an event, through our highly technical minds, then we tend to dismiss it," he said. "We have great difficulty simply standing before the mystery and when we are forced to confront the whole mystery of life, we are unable, like Moses, to just take off our shoes and let the mystery wash over us. And as the mystery washes over us, it tends to unfold before us. But this involves living from our hearts and not from our heads."

He went on to say: "Yet we teach that the way in which we come to faith is by listening with our ears, believing in our hearts and professing with our lips. It's the heart that we struggle with...because it tends to be very difficult to control. The way in which we turn it into a mystery is not through study or research, but rather through prayer—contemplative prayer."

Merton, who wrote prolifically on spirituality and social justice had inspired hundreds of World War II veterans and students who flocked to monasteries across the US after the release of his bestselling autobiography *The Seven Storey Mountain*. He was recognized as one of those rare Western minds that opened up to the Zen experience. In his work, he discusses diverse religious concepts - early monasticism, Russian Orthodox spirituality, the Shakers, and Zen Buddhism – and makes the point that all these studies are driven by the search to grasp life's meaning through a metaphysical awareness.

The truth is that mysticism expresses an emotion and that is not what science can either confirm or deny. Mysticism is about becoming one with God or the Absolute as one pursues the insights to the hidden truths.

In the 19th century, William James (1842-1910), who worked in and between the disciplines of physiology, psychology and philosophy was also an influential proponent of mysticism and proposed that religious experience involves an altogether supernatural domain, somehow inaccessible to science but accessible to the individual human subject.

On "Mysticism" a chapter in his book *The Varieties of Religious Experience*, James offers "four marks which, when an experience has them, may justify us in calling it mystical…" The first is ineffability: "it defies expression…its quality must be directly experienced; it cannot be imparted or transferred to others." Second is a "noetic quality": mystical states present themselves as states of knowledge. Thirdly, mystical states are transient; and, fourth, subjects are passive with respect to them: they cannot control their coming and going."[4]

The later post-reformation period also saw the writings of lay visionaries such as Emanuel Swedenborg and William Blake, and the foundation of mystical movements such as the Quakers. Catholic mysticism continued into the modern period with such figures as Padre Pio and Thomas Merton.[5]

In the modern era, the scope of the notion and practice of mysticism was broadened to include a range of beliefs and ideologies and so mysticism can now be found in all religious traditions, from indigenous and folk religions like shamanism, for example, to organized religions including the Abrahamic faiths and Indian religions.

Judaism has had two main kinds of mysticism: Merkabah mysticism and Kabbalah. The former predated the latter, and was focused on visions, particularly those mentioned in the Book of Ezekiel. It gets its name from the Hebrew word meaning "chariot", a reference to Ezekiel's vision of a fiery chariot composed of heavenly beings. Kabbalah is a set of esoteric teachings meant to explain the relationship between an unchanging, eternal and mysterious *Ein Sof* (no end) and the mortal and finite universe (His creation). Inside Judaism, it forms the foundations of mystical religious interpretation.[6]

India's former Ambassador Pascal Alan Nazareth contends that Swami Vivekananda, the Indian monk who became world renowned after he spoke on Hinduism at the World Parliament of Religions at Chicago in 1893, was primarily responsible for Hinduism's revival in pre-independence India as well in securing for it the status of a world religion and a "spiritual democracy."

In an address he delivered at Benares Hindu University in January 2011, he quoted Swami Vivekananda on what religion actually is: "Religion is not talk, nor doctrine nor theories; nor is it sectarianism. Religion does not consist in erecting temples or building churches or attending public worship. It is the relationship between the individual soul and God. It is not to be found in books or in words or in lectures or in organizations. Religion consists in realization…"

Buddhism, which originated in India, sometime between the 6th and 4th centuries BCE, seeks liberation from the cycle of rebirth by self-control through meditation and morally just behaviour. Some Buddhist paths aim at a gradual development and transformation of the personality toward Nirvana, like the Theravada stages of enlightenment. Others, like the Japanese Rinzai Zen tradition, emphasize sudden insight, but nevertheless also prescribe intensive meditation and self-restraint."[7]

In a narrative told in the passage below, consider how the "eyes of faith" are distinctively independent of the notion of 'belief.'

Joseph Prabhu is a Professor of Philosophy at California State University, Los Angeles, and a member of the Board of Trustees for the Parliament of the World's Religions. In a short note on why he stays with the Catholic church, he firstly recounts the time he was serving at Mass in a small chapel in Calcutta, as the lone altar boy and in the sweltering summer of 1954. "The heat got to me and I fainted and temporarily lost consciousness," he says. "The next thing I know, a diminutive nun in a white sari with a blue border is splashing some water on me, somewhat angrily and irritably telling me to get up, which, of course, I did. I was in no position then to resist the summons of a (future) saint."

He goes on to say: "Such was my introduction to Mother Teresa of the Missionaries of Charity. I got to meet her fairly often as my father and I would assist her in her humanitarian work. But I cannot say that I ever warmed up to her or her version of Catholicism. This had partly to do with the fact that most of my school education was conducted by a remarkable group of Belgian Jesuits at St. Xavier's School, Calcutta, who transmitted a liberal and, for its time, quite enlightened version of the faith."

He says the contrast between the two experiences taught him the vital difference between faith and belief. "The language of faith registers a basic spiritual experience and orientation, which the language of belief tries to formulate in propositional or creedal terms. There is, of course, a dialectical and reciprocal relation between faith and belief, but for me faith is primary, while belief, although important, secondary as far as the spiritual life is concerned."

Professor Prabhu says: "I am critically aware of the shortcomings of the Catholic church, an organization showing itself to be an all-too-human institution with its flagrant abuse of power and its self-aggrandizing-and-protective manner. But the eyes of faith tell me, it (the church) is still, despite its many human failings, the mystical Body of Christ."

He believes the distinction between faith and belief is an important one. "Belief, even though it also involves an element of trust is primarily, although not exclusively, an intellectual matter," he says. "In an age of science, intelligent people will try to make their belief credible and intellectually respectable. But religious faith moves at a different level: more and more I feel it is a divine gift to which one opens oneself, a connection with the Transcendent, which goes beyond the human sphere. I have very little belief that the Catholic Church in its present state of corruption and intoxication with power can transform itself anytime soon. I do have, however, the faith that the Holy Spirit will, over time, purify and redeem the church. That is a faith that is obviously not provable."

He concludes saying: "Science cannot possibly prove or disprove God, because the question of God is not a scientific question at all, but a philosophical or theological one. Science and proof are human concerns, whereas God, by definition, transcends the human order. So human knowledge of God has to come from either divine revelation or religious experience infused with divine grace. If science were to 'prove' God, who would want to pray or to worship such a god? We do not, I hope, worship the Pythagorean Theorem."

In *Seven Storey Mountain,* Merton, narrates the pain that followed on the heels of his father's death. The instinct to pray, he says, can come to even an atheist and while that may not prove the existence of God, at least, it demonstrates the fact that the need to worship Him is driven by our dependent natures. Then he speaks of a life-changing moment, one night in a room with the lights on:

"Suddenly it seemed to me that Father, who had now been dead more than a year, was there with me. The sense of his presence was as vivid and as real and as startling as if he had touched my arm or spoken to me. The whole thing passed in a flash, but in that flash, instantly, I was overwhelmed with a sudden and profound insight into the mystery and corruption of my own soul..."[8] Merton says he was filled with sorrow with what he saw and that the experience brought him to prayer and to a God he had never known "to free him of the thousand terrible things that held him in their slavery."

Mike McHargue in his book *Finding God in the Waves*, narrates his departure from Christianity and how he was able to come back to it through science: "As I stood on the beach in the wee hours of the morning, everything in my surroundings took on that stretched, translucent quality. I could see what I can only call the glory of God on the other side. I felt God with me, in me, and through me. I felt connected with the Source of Life and the Source of All... After it was over, I understood why someone would feel compelled to write about a bush that burned but was not consumed. Or a blinding light on the road to Damascus. Or an angel telling a 14-year old virgin girl she was pregnant with the Son of God."[9] His story almost draws a parallel with the New Testament narrative of Paul's conversion on the road to Damascus.

Now, in the light of these two testimonies presented by two former atheists, who turned to Christianity, this report from PEW research should come as no surprise at all. It's 2014 Religious Landscape Study, reports three-in-ten or 31 percent say they feel a deep sense of spiritual peace and well-being at least weekly. A similar share – approximately thirty five percent, often thinks about the meaning and purpose of life. And roughly half of all atheists – 54 percent frequently feel a deep sense of wonder about the universe, up from 37 percent in 2007. In fact, atheists are more likely than U.S. Christians to say they often feel a sense of wonder about the universe – 54 percent versus 45 percent.[10]

McHargue, posits that spirituality and religion are rooted in the brain in the same way that thoughts and feelings are. His book reveals how the latest in neuroscience, physics and biology help us understand God, faith and ourselves. Scholars of neuroscience are, in fact, proposing that religion is genetically "hardwired" into the human condition, according to recent scientific research.

Consequently, it should come as no surprise that millions of people of faith will today testify to the fact that God has, indeed, been emotionally satisfying, a God who has intervened in the fate and doings of mankind. The brutality of the communist leaders of China, the former Soviet Union, Cambodia, knew it in their gut that the shutting down of churches and mosques would fail to demolish the inner soulful faith of their people. Christians and Muslims worshipped in underground churches and mosques and millions worshipped through a mystical experience.

Professor Dawkins is, understandably, baffled with this growing sense of spirituality that springs forth in mystical ways. He mourns the fact that while great scientists who profess religion become harder to find through the twentieth century, there are nevertheless good scientists who are sincerely religious in the full, traditional sense.

He speaks of Peacocke, Stannard and Polkinghorne who have all either won the Templeton Prize or are on the Templeton Board of Trustees: He writes: "After amicable discussions with all of them, both in public and in private, I remain baffled, not so much by their belief in a cosmic lawgiver of some kind, as by their belief in the details of the Christian religion: resurrection, forgiveness of sin and all." [11]

So why cannot science disprove God? The short answer is that it is because science may be looking for Him in the wrong place.

CHAPTER 7

The Moral Law – Can the world be moral without God?

A monkey and a hyena were walking through the forest when the hyena said:

"Each time I pass by those bushes there a lion jumps out of them and mauls me. I don't know why"

"I'll walk with you this time," said the monkey, "and side with you against the lion." So, they started to walk past the bushes when the lion pounced on the hyena and nearly mauled it to death.

Meanwhile the monkey watched the proceedings from the safety of a tree that he had run up the moment the lion appeared.

"Why didn't you do something to help me?" moaned the hyena. Said the monkey, "You were laughing so much, I thought you were winning."[14]

Anthony de Mello, S.J. *Heart of the Enlightened*

The atheist community has long held the notion that morality is driven by the natural order of human consciousness. It's commonly assumed that people act in ways that are dictated by a moral obligation, that morality commits us to that social consciousness. What this says is that the world can be moral without God. How true is this?

Let's look at the origins of morality and back track 2000 years ago. Until the Edict of Milan in 313, Europe was pagan in its morality and its emperors actually turned a blind eye to the morally shameful practice of infanticide. Slavery which prevailed long before Jesus' time was a flourishing trade and women were subjugated – anti-Samaritan prejudices actually forbade respectable men from speaking to Samaritan women in public.

In a morally bankrupt milieu such as this, Jesus of Nazareth brought about a wind of change that swept across the region and his

Sermon on the Mount introduced a new spiritual morality in the West that was to survive the two millennia and beyond.

Slavery, regarded as an abhorrent social evil in civilized societies today, is as old as the hills. In the book of Genesis (9:25) Noah condemns Canaan (Son of Ham) to perpetual servitude. "Cursed be Canaan! The lowest of slaves will he be to his brothers."

It was practiced in the Near East and Africa several hundred years before the shameful trade crept into Europe. Keep in mind that up until the Edict of Milan, pagan monarchs wielded power in Europe and persecuted Christian societies, blunting Christian societal reform[1], prompting later day critics to point fingers and slight Christian societies for their silent observance of this terrible trade.

But by the year 313, the imperial society in Europe fell apart and its old gods perished in the temples. Christianity seized that moment and changed the moral ethos of nations. The Philemon and Galatian scriptural passages (Galatians 3:28) laid the foundation for the abolition of slavery for the future.

The apostle Paul contrasted the freedom brought by Jesus with the slavery and futility of living under the old law of Judaic practice.[2] His teaching that "there is neither Jew nor Gentile, neither slave nor free, nor is there male and female, for you are all one in Christ Jesus," was revolutionary. *(Galatians 3:28)*

Saint Augustine (354-430) described slavery as being against God's intention and resulting from sin. In *City of God,* he writes: "He did not intend that His rational creature, who was made in His image, should have dominion over anything but the irrational creation, not man over man, but man over the beasts. And hence the righteous men in primitive times were made shepherds of cattle rather than kings of men, God intending thus to teach us what the relative position of the creature is, and what the desert of sin; for it is with justice, we believe, that the condition of slavery is the result of sin. And this is why we do not find the word 'slave' in any part of

Scripture until righteous Noah branded the sin of his son with this name. It is a name, therefore, introduced by sin and not by nature."[3]

That there was Catholic tolerance of and occasional involvement in the slave trade, later, cannot be altogether denied. The New Testament taught slaves to obey their masters,(1 Timothy 6: 1-2) but this was not as an endorsement of slavery, but an appeal to Christian slaves to honor their masters and submit to their suffering for Christ's sake (Ephesians 6:6-8).

The *Beatitudes*, presented by Jesus Christ, in the *Sermon on the Mount* apparently fell on deaf Christian ears many centuries later and the church had been shamed as a result. Slavery in Europe may have seemingly halted in the 14th century but crept into England and in tandem spread to the American colonies.

But history has taught us that great men have risen to the crises of their time and it was just as well that anti-slave trade activism, in England, led by the brave Christian abolitionist, William Wilberforce (24 August 1759 – 29 July 1833) broke through barriers and steered the movement to halt the slave trade. A British politician and philanthropist, Wilberforce was fired with the passion for social reform and in 1787 led the parliamentary campaign against the British slave trade until the passage of the Slave Trade Act of 1807 and later the Slavery Abolition Act which received Royal Ascent on 28 August, 1833 just prior to his death.[4]

Pope John Paul II, in his tenure as head of the Catholic church, has acknowledged this travesty of justice by Christians and apologized on behalf of the church.

So it's fair to say that despite the mistakes of the past, morality in Europe was inspired by Christianity. Cambridge philosopher Elizabeth Anscombe argued, way back in 1958, that the concept of moral obligation in Western philosophy has its roots in Christianity, which perceives of ethics, and morality in terms of laws given by God.

Anscombe's article *Modern Moral Philosophy* stimulated the development of virtue ethics as an alternative to Utilitarianism, Kantian Ethics, and Social Contract theories. Her primary charge in the article is that, as secular approaches to moral theory, they are without foundation. They use concepts such as 'morally ought,' 'morally obligated,' 'morally right,' and so forth that are legalistic and require a legislator as the source of moral authority. In the past God occupied that role, but systems that dispense with God as part of the theory are lacking the proper foundation for meaningful employment of those concepts.[5]

The moral theorist John Stuart Mill has described the concept of moral duty as follows: "We do not call anything wrong unless we mean to imply that a person ought to be punished in some way or other for doing it—if not by law, by the opinion of his fellow creatures; if not by opinion, by the reproaches of his own conscience... It is a part of the notion of duty in every one of its forms that a person may rightfully be compelled to fulfill it. Duty is a thing which may be exacted from a person, as one exacts a debt.[6]

But John Njoroge, who is a member of the speaking team at Ravi Zacharias International Ministries, observes in his piece *Must The Moral Law Have A Law Giver*: "Since obligation is not only a social concept but also an objective one, the existence of God makes the most sense of our experience of morality. Human societies or communities cannot adequately account for moral obligation."[7] That is why the devout believer affirms that the moral law comes from God and is delivered to man by his conscience – man's inner watchdog. This is in sharp contrast to the secular statement which affirms that we do not need God to understand what is right and what is wrong.

But if human societies can account for moral obligation, then why would our societies across the world be driven by deception? Why would the truth be so elusive? Why in godless societies do we see sexual assaults carried out in complete defiance of societal approval?

What about the brutality of war, the Holocaust, the torture of prisoners?

That man's inner voice is the moral conscience and the driving force compelling moral action, is an insight that law courts all of the world accept and therefore rely on that divinely driven compass to extract the truth when a believer delivers it with his hand on the Holy Book of his faith. It tells you that man is compelled to fulfill that moral duty before God and not before society.

Njoroge says it is often assumed that reason by itself is adequate to give us all we want in terms of knowing and acting upon our moral obligations. "What is moral to do, the claim goes, is what is reasonable to do. But although morality is, indeed, reasonable, the relationship between the two is not as clear cut as the foregoing claim implies. It is one thing to have good reasons to do something and quite another to be obligated to do it. Having reasons to perform an action does not necessarily imbue one with the kind of obligation morality requires."[8]

It is important to understand why moral obligation is a dictate of an inner voice and not driven solely by reason. Scientists have now begun to study God by observing how religious experiences affect the human brain. Some leading neuroscientists have coined a term "neurotheology" to describe this discipline. Neurotheology, we are told, doesn't try to prove or disprove God.

"It's a pragmatic field entirely devoted to studying the effects religion and spirituality have on human brains," McHargue observes. The two basic brain networks that work together to make God real in the minds of humans like us are, understandably, complex and explain much about our faith. "It explains why people with higher activity in their frontal lobes will be drawn to apologetics or theology – they want to know how God works. On the other hand, people with higher activity in their limbic systems will know God through feelings and have little concern with rational justifications for God's existence. They know God because they feel God,"[9] he says.

But outside the disciplines of neurotheology, how do you counter God. C.S. Lewis, in his book *Mere Christianity* provides an excellent case for the moral law versus the instinctive impulse.

"Supposing you hear a cry for help from a man in danger, you will probably feel two desires – one a desire to give help (due to your herd instinct), the other a desire to keep out of danger. But you will find inside you, in addition to the two impulses, a third thing which tells you that you ought to follow the impulse to help and suppress the impulse to run away. Now this thing that judges between two instincts...cannot itself be either of them. The moral Law tells us the tune we have to play; our instincts are merely the keys.[10]

The foregoing perspective easily dismisses as fallacy the claim that societal construct is the compelling force driving moral obligation. That claim cannot stand as the truth. That is because we do not live in a perfect world or in a puritanical society. If we did, the evil we see around us would not be as ubiquitous as it is: a car rams into innocent crowds during white supremacist marches in Charlottesville in the United States; a van ploughs into pedestrians on Westminister Bridge in London. Across the world, we see autocratic or tyrannical regimes pushing forth an amoral agenda, carried out by civil servants who see obedience to these amoral dictates as societal obligations. A culture of deceit sweeps across the political ethos of many nations.

Furthermore, there cannot be a uniform moral law for mankind if that morality was founded on a societal construct whose foundation is built upon secular or cultural traditions. In a secular world, we see relativism as the foundation for moral judgement about what is right and what is wrong. That equation is dependent on a perspective. The truth is relative. The pre-determinist holds the view that if God is truly omnipotent, then He is the fountainhead of all of man's actions. That's relativism again. How is man to be guided by a moral law that's founded on a societal construct, where cultural, religiously diverse tradition, political dictates and ideology shape that society. That – as a collective argument – makes a convincing case for why the universal moral law can come from the moral lawgiver alone.

Njoroge points out that the demands of morality frequently conflict with our self-interests in a way that suggests that they transcend mere individual or societal conventions. "If we were solely responsible for assigning moral obligations to ourselves, why would we make them so difficult to fulfill, and why do we keep on trying to meet them when we have proven that we are incapable of doing so, perfectly? Our very struggle in this area shows that we recognize the transcendent, otherworldly source of our moral obligations.[11]

Notwithstanding the fact that we see unconscionable and amoral action in everyday life that sometimes rocks the foundation of peace on the planet, there should be no denying of the fact that all of humanity is endowed with a conscience that points the way to truth. The conscience holder, of course, is free to shut up his whistleblower, but the whistle goes off regardless. Clearly, if you are looking for evidence of a God who cares about you, all you need to do is listen to the voice within you that points the way to truth.

Lewis provides another perspective: "If there was a controlling power outside the universe, it could not show itself to us as one of the facts inside the universe -no more than the architect of a house could actually be a wall or staircase or fireplace in that house. The only way in which we could expect it to show itself would be inside ourselves as an influence or a command trying to get us to behave in a certain way. And that is just what we do find inside ourselves."[12]

Indeed, free will plays havoc when confronted with the voice of conscience and that is at the heart of all evil. Christian violence in the Crusades, the Holocaust in World War II; the communist-atheist killings in China, the former Soviet Union, Cambodia; Buddhist violence in Myanmar and Sri Lanka or terrorist violence by Islamic extremists across the world are evidence of that very fact—a consequence of free will and its abuse.

Njoroge observes: "We know that some things are really wrong. Other things are really right, and there is an objective moral standard that helps us differentiate between the two. We also sense quite strongly that this can only be true if God exists. Morality is indeed grounded in God. Once one begins to realize that morality is not relative, that it cannot be grounded in biological evolution, and that it cannot be fully explained on the basis of social conventions or individual taste, one immediately feels drawn to the conclusion that God must exist."[13]

So, can we be moral without God? The next time you've done something seriously wrong, listen to the voice within you in a silent moment. Social organization cannot erase the guilt in you because the state's criteria of right and wrong is built not on a morality principle but on social and political responsibility. That was the distinction that separated State and Church. So, despite the fact that secular laws of the state may deem no wrong on your part in the exercise of your right to choose, the truth will torment you. It's that third eye of the heart that troubles you. The notion that morality is dictated by moral obligation and is driven by social consciousness is fallacious as this chapter has sought to prove. Listen to your inner voice alone and come up with an answer to the question: 'can we be moral without God?'

CHAPTER 8

Can suffering and death be designs of a caring God?

In 1348, the bubonic plague or Black Death swept across Europe, wiping out a third of humanity at the time, or approximately 75 million lives.[1] The 1918 Spanish flu infected 500 million people around the world, including people on remote Pacific islands and in the Arctic and resulted in the deaths of 50 to 100 million or five percent of the world's population.[2] In the last century, World War 1 saw casualties of 40 million lives and World War II was the deadliest military conflict in history. An estimated total of 70-85 million people perished, which was about three percent of the 1940 world population.[3] On a less appalling scale, natural calamity from tsunamis, droughts, earthquakes, heat waves, floods and landslides have wiped away hundreds of thousands of people in the last 20 years. Indeed, these have all been natural calamities, but it's perfectly natural to ask 'why does a loving God allow suffering and death.' Whereas, the short answer is that no one is going to pretend to know the mind of God, science and theology can, at best, make some sense of why suffering and death prevail.

Darwin wrote in *The Origin of Species* "In looking at nature it is most necessary to keep the foregoing considerations always in mind, never to forget that every single organic being around us may be said to be striving to the utmost to increase in numbers; that each lives by a struggle at some period of its life, that heavy destruction inevitably falls either on the young or old during each generation or at recurrent intervals."[4]

Suffering, as theologians agree, is inevitable in everyone's lifetime as a consequence of the fall of man – a theological position presented in the foregoing pages of this chapter.

But what's increasingly troubling really, is that outside the realm of natural calamities, suffering and death are an everyday occurrence on our planet and all of that ongoing tragedy is provoked by mankind's lust and greed, notions of supremacy and the drive to conquer, bringing into the world poverty and strife, hateful ideology, violence and destruction, conflict and war, often orchestrated for the cause of nationhood and religion, both of which are accidents of birth. It is we who have brought guns and bombs into the fray pitting people of faiths and cultures in combat for the disruption of peace and destruction of our world. The senseless brutality we see in our cities is primed by our own moral decadence, hatreds - often ideological, at other times racial and bigoted, driven by supremacist illusions and imperialist ambitions.

On September 11, 2001, Islamic jihadists hijacked planes and crashed them into the Twin Towers in New York. The world watched the unfolding tragedy in shock as people jumped out of windows to their death. The official casualty toll was 2,996 dead and more than 6,000 others wounded. At the time, Americans were all asking the same question: "Why does God allow tragedy and suffering."

The American Christian evangelist Billy Graham, speaking at the National Cathedral in Washington D.C. on September 14, 2001 three days after the 9/11 tragedy, told crowds gathered to hear him: "I have to confess I do not know the answer. The story does not end with the cross, for Easter points us beyond the tragedy of the cross to the empty tomb. It tells us that there is hope for eternal life, for Christ has conquered evil and death and hell. Yes, there is hope."[5] Graham went on to say: "I have to accept, by faith, that God is sovereign, and that He is a God of love and mercy and compassion in the midst of suffering. The Bible says God is not the author of evil. In 1 Thessalonians 2:7 the Bible talks about the mystery of iniquity."

But why cannot God intervene? It is fallacious to presume that God would bestow us with free will and withhold it at the same time. The Genesis story of the fall of Adam is about Satan luring Eve with the notion that in rejecting God, they could set up on their own and be free. Theologians agree that with that hopeless bid came the trials and tribulations in human history and all of the morass that permeates since.

So cannot God destroy evil altogether? Let's see. Daniel Defoe, author of *Robinson Crusoe*, narrates a conversation with his man Friday which provides an insight to the question: "Well," says Friday, "but you say God is so strong, so great; is He not much strong, much might as the devil?"

"Yes, yes," says I, "Friday, God is stronger than the devil—God is above the devil, and therefore we pray to God to tread him down under our feet, and enable us to resist his temptations and quench his fiery darts."

"But," says he again, "if God much stronger, much might as the wicked devil, why God no kill the devil, so make him no more do wicked?"

I was strangely surprised at this question; and, after all, though I was now an old man, yet I was but a young doctor, and ill qualified for a casuist or a solver of difficulties; and at first I could not tell what to say; so I pretended not to hear him, and asked him what he said; but he was too earnest for an answer to forget his question, so that he repeated it in the very same broken words as above.

By this time I had recovered myself a little, and I said, "God will at last punish him severely; he is reserved for the judgment, and is to be cast into the bottomless pit, to dwell with everlasting fire." This did not satisfy Friday; but he returns upon me, repeating my words, "'*Reserve at last!*' me no understand—but why not kill the devil now; not kill great ago?"

"You may as well ask me," said I, "why God does not kill you or me, when we do wicked things here that offend Him—we are preserved to repent and be pardoned." He mused some time on this. "Well, well," says he, mighty affectionately, "that well—so you, I, devil, all wicked, all preserve, repent, God pardon all." [6]

In choosing to empower man with free will, God chose to witness his people deal with the consequences of their actions. But while He gave man the free will to choose, he did not part with the free will to will and in holding tight to those reins, has pre-empted the complete destruction and annihilation of the planet.

In recent tragedies, God's intervention was transparent. Psalm 91: 7 tells us: "A thousand shall fall at thy side, and ten thousand at thy right hand; but it shall not come nigh thee." The random stories posted online, after the 9/11 tragedy, speak of strange coincidences that kept people alive on 9/11: like the man whose turn it was to bring donuts, the woman whose alarm clock did not go off, someone missed a bus, the car that did not start and so forth. The people who were not in the towers by accident may have regarded that escape as God's intervention.

Suffering is a given. In his Deer Park sermon, Buddha expounded his first teaching of the Four Noble Truths, which explain the problem of suffering and misery in the world and offer a solution. Those four noble truths are: 1. There is suffering 2. There is a cause of suffering 3. There is cessation of suffering 4. There is a path to the cessation of suffering.[7]

Speaking to delegates at the third Spiritual Diversity Conference that I hosted in Halifax in 2016, Shastri Robert Gailey, quoted Sakyong Mipham Rinpoche, a Buddhist teacher, as saying: "At this time, great confusion and suffering exists because humanity cannot simply be. The first step in unraveling conflict with the world is making friends with ourselves... making peace with ourselves."[8]

The theological response to the question about why God allows suffering and death is addressed also through revealed Christian scripture: The New Testament calls death "the last enemy" (1 Corinthians 15:26) and "the wages of sin" (Romans 6:23).

So, how does Christian theology account for sin being the harbinger of death? In Romans 5:12 we are told that as a result of his sin, Adam and his descendants acquired a sin nature and lost the power of contrary choice. So man can no longer go against his sin nature and therefore is saddled with sin. (Psalm 51:5, Jeremiah 17:9, Romans 7:15–25). Consequently, death and suffering are the penalty for sin.

The Bible informs us that Adam was the first of creation and therefore head of the human race, representing all of mankind. The apostle Paul says that we sin "in Adam", after the likeness of Adam (Romans 5:12–19). In other words, we inherit Adam's sin and are "by nature children of wrath" (Ephesians 2:3). Theologians therefore agree that with Adam's rebellion against God, all of his descendents are regarded as people wanting a life without God. The theological deduction thus concludes that since God is the author of life, death is the natural penalty of wanting life without its Creator.

In Romans 1:18-32 we are told that God lets things fall apart to give us a sense of a godless world. But in the book of Daniel, (Chapter 3), we are told of Shadrach, Meshach, and Abednego walking into an intensely blazing furnace—yet coming out without even the smell of smoke on their clothes. That's a glimpse of a Godly world. Miracles are not a myth. Let me tell you what I know.

On 8 July 2018, life's nasty challenge came down on us like a ton of bricks. Teresa, my dear wife was diagnosed with third stage ovarian cancer. I put on a brave face while family and friends were at her bedside in that hospital ward, pale and horrified as the diagnosis was pronounced. But when they left in despair, in a private moment with Teresa, I burst into tears. She choked for a brief moment and then told me: "It does not matter. It's just you that I am thinking of...and of course, my children as well." That was the saddest moment of our lives.

In the following weeks, intensive investigations got underway. Then one morning, Teresa's body temperature shot up to 38.4°C and we rushed her to the emergency unit of the QEII hospital in Halifax. The doctors second guessed it was pneumonia, because her lungs were jammed with fluid. But radiology rejected the diagnosis and doctors were temporarily foxed with the problem. So she was put on broad spectrum antibiotics. In the couple of weeks before 8 July, Teresa had lost some fifteen pounds; her spirit in private was drooping.

A couple of weeks later she was at the cancer centre of the QEII again for the first chemo treatment at 9:00 in the morning. Who was to say how that would go? She was doing fine at first, then ten minutes into the treatment, her condition got precarious all at once. The nurses were put on high alert. "High risk" they said. Teresa's heart beat shot up suddenly and she was struggling for every gasp of breath. The nurses scurried around for an oxygen cylinder. My daughters and I were cold with fear and as gloom descended upon us they distracted me, because the silence was eerie, and the sound of the clock clicking was annoying. But ten long minutes later, calm gradually descended and Teresa began to breathe normally. And so did we. That was scary. That night I suffered nightmares of the worst order. The following morning, a tube was inserted into Teresa's rib cage and 1.2 litres of that lung fluid was drained out.

On the Sunday of that week, my son and I drove to church to celebrate Mass. I was spiritually overwhelmed as the liturgy sank in. My son watched despairingly as he saw me weep in silence. Then he put his hand around me and said nothing. A young priest delivered the homily that Sabbath day. But I clung to the one line that provided comfort. "Faith," he said, "is trust and submission." He was saying, I think, that neither trust nor submission can stand alone in faith. They go hand in hand. I wrote it down somewhere in the folds of my heart, and peace streamed in. Then in a quiet moment, during the elevation of bread and wine that was soon to be transformed in Christian spiritual awakeness, into the body and blood of Jesus Christ, I contemplated on another spiritual truth delivered at a homily by a Franciscan priest in a chapel at a hamlet in Goa, a tourist haven on

India's southwestern coast. He was speaking at the Good Friday Mass a couple of years ago and in his concluding remarks said. "My dear friends, remember this: "The next time there is a Good Friday in your life, keep in mind, Easter – is only a hop, skip and jump away." Easter is the celebration of the resurrection of Jesus from the dead.

In the middle of September, Teresa had to prepare for her third chemo treatment. In the intervening time, family and dear friends from across the planet stormed heaven to supplicate for her speedy recovery, while she spent her days on a bed at home communicating with God through notes on the pages of her journal. "Lord, I do not know what you have in store for me, so I cannot pray for my own recovery," she wrote in one of her notes. "But be compassionate to the others I know who are touched by cancer. Show them your healing hand, Lord." She ruminated on her early years recalling the time when she was called to be brave, at the start line of the 100-metre sprint, the moment of adversity in her teens and then moments in good times and in bad. Teresa's model of prayer to the Lord was a selfless one.

On September 10, my dear wife sailed through that third chemo treatment with flying colours and when three weeks later her blood report landed on the desk of the chief oncologist, he jumped off his chair and dashed out euphoric - to see us waiting in the clinic for answers - just like the ancient Greek mathematician and inventor, Archimedes, did many hundreds of years ago jumping out of his bath tub and sprinting naked on the streets proclaiming Eureka. Teresa's ovarian cancer cell count had fallen from 790 to 35.

Was that a catharsis? Was this our Easter? No, not yet! On 18 October, the hospital surgeons carried out a hysterectomy procedure on Teresa and six hours later the doctor, speaking to me on the phone told me the surgeons in the operating room were foxed and bewildered. "None of us were able to see any trace of cancer," she whispered in a low voice. "Robin this is great news." A couple of nurses standing around me watched with joy as I got teary eyed. Are miracles a myth? Really?

But it's not over, until it's over, they say. Three more chemo treatments were to follow and with it, in tow, would come the trauma and anxiety of chemotoxity. Who was to say what was in store, as fervent prayers and supplication stormed heaven again. My son and daughters flew down intermittently from different parts of the world - so did my siblings and extended family from far and near converge on our home to assist in post-operation trauma, general nursing, the administration of clot-pre-emption injections and spiritual care. Family, grandkids and dear friends went out on a limb to care for Teresa.

Then on 31 December 2018, Teresa underwent her last chemo treatment. A new year was about to break within hours and excitement rent the air as champagne bottles stood ready on bar counters in homes waiting to be popped. At 4:00 p.m. that evening, the doctors signed off on medical papers confirming Teresa's remission status and in utter joy she took possession of that celebratory bell in the chemo centre and held it aloft ringing it with mad joy. Then hours before the new year dawned, she and I gathered with family at home and glorified the Lord. Was that our Easter? Yes, indeed it was. Teresa had ended her battle with cancer.

In April this year, my sister Lorna and her spouse Tony celebrated their 50th wedding anniversary in Toronto, their new home. At the podium, responding to the toast, she began by saying: "Let me testify to a miracle that unfolded early in our married life. I was barely twenty two at the time and Vimla, our daughter, was a toddler then, when I was struck by a sickness that bewildered the best of India's doctors. My health was protean and the diagnosis was nebulous. I was wasting away through four long months of struggle on a hospital bed and had been reduced to feather weight. The doctors held out no hope and gloom spread. But in my heart, trust in and submission to the Lord God was unshakeable. Then something happened as I waited at death's door. On the morning of the feast day

63

of the Holy Spirit, after months of wasting away on a hospital bed, I jumped out of that bed and walked across corridors to see fellow patients. Hospital staff were aghast. Was this a ghost? Well, no. God had revealed His merciful hand in my recovery. So even today at 72, I live to praise and glorify God."

So, there is hope. 1 Corinthians 15:20 – 26 tells us "But Christ has indeed been raised from the dead, the first fruits of those who have fallen asleep. For since death came through a man, the resurrection of the dead comes also through a man. For as in Adam all die, so in Christ all will be made alive." There is grandeur in this view of life.

The apostle Paul, who was struck down by lightning on the road to Damascus while pursuing his mission of persecution of the Christians, rose up and saw the light. That was a life-changing event. Paul then went on to preach the gospel of Christ to nations across Europe and became the angel of Christian evangelisation. But in the end, Paul suffered torture, beatings, imprisonment, stoning and finally execution. His letters reveal that Jesus Christ's resurrection was the key to his making sense of his suffering. In his letter to the Corinthians (1 Corinthians 15:14, 19) he says: "And if Christ has not been raised, our preaching is useless and so is your faith. More than that, we are then found to be false witnesses about God, for we have testified about God that he raised Christ from the dead. But he did not raise him if, in fact, the dead are not raised."

It is common to hear the despairing wail of those disillusioned by God's conspicuous absence in the midst of trial and tribulation. People have turned away from God when tragedy has struck that fatal blow. Darwin gave up his practice of Christianity after the death of his daughter. These impulsive responses apparently come from a superficial perspective of the Creator and loving God whose mind we cannot pretend to know, save for the fact that he has revealed His hand in the work of creation and in the saving grace bestowed on the sick, the dying, the mute, the repressed and the marginalised.

Perhaps it's not uncommon to reason that the presence of trial and tribulation, the evil of war and destruction, oppression and injustice upon the weak and innocent would be adequate proof that a loving creator does not exist. But consider the fact that despite the trial and tribulation, the evil of war and destruction, oppression and injustice upon the weak and innocent, driven by the abuse of free will, we are every day witness to how the human race counters evil with good, war with peace, oppression with justice, hatred with love. In our time, we have seen how the mighty have fallen, blood thirsty dictatorships have crumbled, the oppressed have found refuge, the poor are fed and hatred has been blunted.

Merton suggests that this would never have been possible without the merciful love of God, pouring out His grace upon mankind. That is because there can, at least, be no doubt about the authors of hate, avarice and injustice, all of which sow the seeds of war and destruction.

The fact that there is suffering and death, is a crusading matter for atheists making a point that there cannot be a loving God who would preside over pain and tribulation. What is probably troubling for the secularist, however, is why despite the ubiquity of pain and tribulation, billions of believers on the planet yet cling to the Creator for refuge.

Secularists and critics of religion have posed the question at various times about why a belief in a divine and omnipotent Creator who has promised a glorious afterlife, not make the devout religionist content and peaceful. But are secularists content and peaceful, for goodness sake? Evil in the world is troubling. A human heart cannot witness suffering and death and not be touched by it. The news montage on any ordinary day can be very terrifying: *North Korea fires missile over Japan! Catastrophic floods rising in Houston! Iran building missiles in Syria! Rohingya women weep on border! Shock and fear amid South Africa cannibalism case!*

In truthfulness, can anyone, secularist or theist, stand by and watch one's child being torn away from them? How would anyone, secularist or theist, have reacted should the Holocaust have unfolded in front of their eyes? Would anyone, secularist or theist, not be touched by the 9/11 tragedy, watching people jump to their death as the towers were burning? Did anyone, secularist or theist, sleep well at night after the day the young Syrian boy was washed ashore somewhere in Europe while escaping an ugly war raging in his country? Evil in the world is troubling and when grief and gloom spread, the heart is sad and broken. In truthfulness, can secularists declare that they are anymore happy than the other man on the street?

Jesus wept at the tomb of Lazarus, when he saw his sisters Martha and Mary in utter bereavement. Death, in itself, is a moment of joy to the spiritual individual. It recalls the Easter promise of the empty tomb. But grief is another thing. Yet if God has lovingly promised his people a haven for eternity, why does such a belief not make His faithful happy? Well, for clarity, the story of the apostle Peter sinking at sea must be told.

When Jesus saw his disciples on a boat in trouble with the winds, he came walking upon the water to comfort them. His disciples seeing him approach from afar in the night, were afraid. Then Peter called out saying: "If it be thou, bid me come unto thee." And Jesus said "Come." So Peter got off the boat and walked. But when he realized the winds were boisterous, he began to sink. Jesus, then, stretched out his hand, saying: "O ye of little faith, why did you doubt?"

The frailty of the human condition pre-empts the serenity we seek. The human soul cannot sustain a passage of peace for as long as suffering permeates. The irony is that suffering is a vicious cycle. You and I are a part of that. It's we who have designed weapons and built an industry out of it to fire our economies. It's we who promote hate, indulge in deceit, greed, lust and cruelty, oppression and injustice – all of which are the primers of violence. It's we who decide to go to war fighting over nationhood and our faith. It's we who have abused the gift of free will to bring evil into the world.

Merton notes in *The Seven Storey Mountain*: "I shall never forget a casual remark Father happened to make, in which he told me of St. Peter's betrayal of Christ and how, hearing the cock crow, Peter went out and wept bitterly..." The guilt that comes from breaking the moral law haunts and torments the soul. Judas kissed Jesus on the cheek to signal to the assassins that he was the man they were hounding. Then he hung himself on a tree after his betrayal. So as Merton observes: "It is his own existence, his own being, that is at once the subject and the source of his pain and his very existence and consciousness is his greatest torture."[9]

Hate and greed and lust and cruelty and oppression, injustice, betrayal, in the ultimate analysis, make all of us sad.

Professor Dawkins in his preface to the book *The God Delusion* urges his readers to imagine, with John Lennon, a world with no religion. That, he imagines would be a world free of the brutal wars of the last couple of centuries, the crusades and the suicide bombing, witch-hunts and persecutions, honour killings and beheadings. But a world without religion was shamefully witnessed in Stalin and Lenin's Soviet Union, Pol Pot's Cambodia and Mao's China in the last century. These were the regions of the world where religion was ruthlessly struck down and replaced with militant atheism. Christians and Muslims worshipped in underground churches and mosques. Then before long, *Glasnost* and *Perestroika* changed everything. So, would you imagine a world without religion?

In his erudite article *Why does a loving God allow death and suffering*, Dr. Jonathan Sarfati of Creation Ministries International, says that for an atheist to complain that the Christian God is 'evil', he must provide a standard of good and evil by which to judge Him. "But if we are simply evolved pond scum, as a consistent atheist must believe, where can we find an objective standard of right and wrong? Our ideas of right and wrong, under this system, are merely artefacts of some chemical processes that occur in the brain, which happened to confer survival advantage on our alleged ape-like ancestors," Sarfati observes. "But the motions in Hitler's brain obeyed the same chemical laws as those in Mother Teresa's, so on what grounds are the latter's actions 'better' than the former's? Also, why should the terrorist attack slaying thousands of people in New York be more terrible than a frog killing thousands of flies?"[10]

Sarfati goes on to point out that evolutionist Jaron Lanier had demonstrated the problem, saying, "There's a large group of people who simply are uncomfortable with accepting evolution because it leads to what they perceive as a moral vacuum, in which their best impulses have no basis in nature."[11]

Life, suffering and death can only begin to present meaning when you see the goodness of God pass you by in the little miracles that unfold: the love of a soul mate, an act of deep compassion, the knowledge that suffering can be fleeting and death is the last enemy that the resurrection of Christ puts paid to.

O death where is thy sting!

CHAPTER 9

Is religion the cause of all the evil in the world?

A philosopher who had only one pair of shoes asked the cobbler
to repair them for him while he waited.
"It's closing time," said the cobbler, "so it won't be possible for me to repair them
just now. Why don't you come for them tomorrow?"
"I have only one pair of shoes and it won't be possible for me to walk without shoes."
"Very well, I shall lend you a used pair for the day."
"What! Wear someone else's shoes? What do you take me for?"
"Why should you object to having someone else's shoes on your feet when you
don't mind carrying other people's ideas in your head?"[9]

Anthony de Mello, S.J. *Heart of the Enlightened*

Evil in the world cannot, in theory, come from religion. Think of a child in arms strapped to a bomb somewhere in Nigeria. Can that possibly come from the Creator? Can that come from true religion which proposes to be the moral compass? It comes from fallen people as a consequence of God's gift of free will to mankind.

There is a sense that the secularist who dismisses religion as an opiate is quick to dismiss the Creator alongside, as if the two were along the same twain. They do this because people of religion, like all others, fall from grace at some point or the other, dropping their moral high-ground, ceding to human error and thus shaking the edifice of their religious institutions. It is just another convenient allegation to discredit divinity and hang the argument on a guilt cross. The argument against a Creator God, is a separate twain. Nonetheless, this chapter must address the question: Is religion the cause of all the evil in the world?

In the drive to denigrate religion, critics have pointed to religious and fundamental theology that have introduced dogmatism into moral teaching, thus sometimes provoking doctrine conflict among faith groups; promoting superstition, incarcerating witches and perpetuating the concept of damnation in hell; and condemning homosexuality and abortion.

Critics point to holy wars – the Crusades, the Inquisitions, the condemnation of blasphemers, the incarceration of journalists and scientists as well as the emergence of suicide bombers who, exploiting religion, have struck terror in the world. In recent times, critics also point to some cases of pedophilia in the Catholic church, the suppression of liberal thought and the sustained neglect of ignorance to perpetuate the patronage of its followers.

A major stumbling block for many earnest seekers is the compelling evidence throughout history that terrible things have been done in the name of religion. The condemnation is slapped on virtually all faiths including those that argue for compassion and non-violence among their principal tenets.

So how do you account for the times when terrible things have been done in the name of religion? The simple truth is that all of us have fallen short of the moral law. The Church is made up of fallen people just as other religionists might admit to the stain brought to their institutions. The failings of the church down through the centuries have nothing to do with the profound teachings of Christ – examine the *Sermon on the Mount*.

Jesus told crowds who gathered to hear him: *"Blessed are the poor in spirit, for theirs is the kingdom of heaven. Blessed are they that mourn, for they shall be comforted. Blessed are the meek for they shall inherit the earth. Blessed are they who do hunger and thirst after righteousness, for they shall be filled. Blessed are the merciful, for they shall obtain mercy. Blessed are the pure in heart for they shall see God. Blessed are the peacemakers for they shall be called the children of God. Blessed are they which are persecuted for righteousness sake, for theirs is the kingdom of heaven."*

Jesus Christ taught his disciples some of the most revolutionary truths ever uttered:

"But to you who are listening I say: Love your enemies, do good to those who hate you, bless those who curse you, pray for those who mistreat you. If someone slaps you on one cheek, turn to them the other also. If someone takes your coat, do not withhold your shirt from them. Give to everyone who asks you, and if anyone takes what belongs to you, do not demand it back. Do to others as you would have them do to you." (Luke 6: 27-31)

The American novelist Vonnegut always spoke in awe when he commented on Jesus Christ. "I say of Jesus, as all humanists do: if what he said is good, and so much of it is absolutely beautiful, what does it matter if he was God or not?" Then he goes on to say: "But if Christ hadn't delivered the *Sermon on the Mount*, with its message of mercy and pity, I wouldn't want to be a human being. I'd just as soon be a rattle snake."[1]

Albert Einstein is reported to have told the poet George Viereck, in an interview, that despite being a Jew, he is enthralled by the luminous figure of the Nazarene. Then, when prodded about the historical existence of Jesus, he declared that "No one can truly read the gospels without feeling the actual presence of Jesus, because his personality pulsates in every word."[2]

But along the way in history, this Christian *Magna Carta* had sadly fallen by the wayside and the only saving grace is that Christians now accept that they are a fallen people.

India's towering freedom fighter, Mohandas K. Gandhi, is known to have said: "I like your Christ, I do not like your Christians. Your Christians are so unlike your Christ." He was probably right. A small section of the world's Catholic population today are content Sunday Catholics - distinguished by their strict observance of the traditional and written law with pretensions to superior sanctity. The narrative below is a common but convincing example of that hypocritical label.

On a holiday in Mumbai, a couple of years ago, my wife and I were hosted by a sibling whose apartment overlooked a very cosmopolitan Indian society.

That week on a Sunday morning, I had poured myself a coffee and sat by the window. An irate young Christian man was yelling abuse at a Hindu gentleman who had by accident dented a small portion of his car in the parking lot. The dent was insignificant but the gentleman apologized and promised to make good on the repair work and pay for all costs. But Louis, the owner of the car with that insignificant dent, would take no apologies. He spat out some even more malicious abuse at the gentleman and told him finally. "You know, I am in a hurry to get to the 9:00 am Sunday Mass. But for that, I would have been merciless with you." Then he scooted off on a scooter. My immediate reaction was: "Thank God for religion." But that was tongue-in-cheek sarcasm prompted by my disgust of this vile behaviour from a professed Christian.

Louis had apparently not laid a hand on a copy of the *Beatitudes*, nor listened at all when it was read out at Sunday Mass. He was content placing his offering in the Sunday collection box, secure in the knowledge that salvation would not be denied to him. This man is a sample of so many other church goers who have ignored a plea for a dime from panhandlers on a Sunday morning, because that dime had to be dropped into the Sunday collection box. So, indeed, Gandhi was perhaps right.

In his book *Darwin's Angel*, Cornwell provides a comforting observation. He makes a poignant point about the acknowledgement of fallenness which enables Christians to rise up and start again because the creed is a God-centered one, starkly distinguished from man-centred ideologies, which when they fail are abandoned in the garbage bins of history.

In recent years, the paedophilia scandal in the Church, has shocked and shamed devout and inspired Christians. But the aftermath of news reports, while appalling, is shameful as well. The random abandoning of the faith by Christians is a sad commentary on how superfluous faith had made its way into the corridors of the Christian church. Why would Christians walk away from the church of Christ every time a news report flags a paedophile case involving a priest? Do you curse the sun, if the night has driven you to steal? What has the sin of a fallen priest got to do with your abiding love of and trust in a loving Creator.

So, let's now go back to the question about how do you account for the times when terrible things have been done in the name of religion. How do you account for the violence by Islamic suicide bombers carried out in God's name? Dr. Jamal Badawi, a member of the Islamic Judicial Council of North America, the European Council for ISTA and Research and the International Union of Muslim Scholars, told delegates at the 2011 Spiritual Diversity Conference I hosted in Halifax: "The Qur'an confirms God's revelation that: If anyone slays a human being, unless it be punishment for murder or for spreading mischief on earth, it shall be as though he had slain all humankind, whereas if anyone saves a life, it shall be as though he had saved the lives of all mankind." (Qur'an: 5: 32).

How do you account for the violence unleashed by Buddhists in Sri Lanka and Myanmar although Buddhism preaches compassion and that all life is sacred? In his address to the first Spiritual Diversity Conference I had convened in Halifax in 2011, Royal Pandit Bhikkhu Saranapala, Rector, College of Buddhist Studies at the West End Buddhist Cultural Centre in Ontario, told delegates: "In Buddhism, the practice of Dhamma is to embrace all sentient beings as sentient beings. All life is sacred. Buddha did not only refer to man, but all forms of life, visible and invisible who feel pain and suffering in his umbrella of love."

So it's just as well that in the last twenty five years, the Church of Rome has apologized for almost all of its gross mistakes. Since his election in 2013, Pope Francis has adopted a hard line on pedophilia in the Catholic Church and urged bishops around the world to adopt a zero-tolerance approach to clerical sex abuse.

Pope John Paul II offered several apologies as well. During his long reign as Pope (1978-2005) he apologized to Muslims killed by Crusaders; others convicted by the Spanish Inquisition; to Jews for the silence of many Catholics during the Holocaust; to women for violation of their rights and their denigration, and just about everyone who had allegedly suffered at the hands of the Catholic Church over the years.

As Pope, he officially made public apologies for over 100 of these wrongdoings, including: the legal process around 1633 on the Italian scientist and philosopher Galileo Galilei, himself a devout Catholic; Catholics' involvement with the African slave trade; the Church's role in burnings at the stake and the religious wars that followed the Protestant Reformation; the injustices committed against women and several other wrongdoings.[3]

Like Islam, Hinduism, Judaism, or any religion with roots deep in history, Christianity has myriad misdeeds to live down, venerable traditions to live up to, and proven principles, by which people can live responsibly and learn the gratitude at the heart of all true religion.[4]

But not all of the troubles presented by critics of religion stand the test of truth. Critics have pointed to doctrinal interpretations that have triggered political conflict in many parts of the world and which have stood in the way of peaceful reconciliation. The Northern Ireland conflict and the Bosnian war in Europe have been blamed on religious intolerance when, in fact, the conflicts were primarily political and nationalistic, with an ethnic and sectarian dimension.

Imperialism, militarism and nationalism were the principal primers of World War 1. The desire of the Slavic peoples in Bosnia and Herzegovina to be part of Serbia and no longer part of Austria-Hungary brought about an essentially nationalistic and ethnic revolt that finally pulled the trigger on Archduke Ferdinand. The assassination of Ferdinand led to Austria-Hungary declaring war on Serbia and the rest is history.

The priming force driving Europe to World War II was revanchism, the burning desire to reverse territorial losses and Adolf Hitler's desire for a pure Aryan citizenry. Now what had religion to do in these two world wars that swallowed up scores of millions of lives.

Christopher Hitchens in his book *God is not Great-Religion Poisons Everything,*[5] puts the blame on religion for being the provocateur and fomenter of the partitioning of India in 1947. He points a finger at Mahatma Gandhi's politics that polarized India, pitting Muslims against Hindus; his distaste of modernity and embrace of the village-dominated, spiritually-driven Hindu society.

Gandhi may have rejected modernity and advocated a spiritual society. But India's other great intellectual, Pandit Jawaharlal Nehru, who led the country to independence had by then proclaimed that India lived in its villages. A noble truth that is even today somewhat true.

The freedom struggle in India was a political movement and Gandhi had been acknowledged worldwide then, for his civil disobedience and non-violence movements which actually worked to drive the British out of India. Gandhi and Nehru had led this freedom struggle and while Gandhi was looking to an agrarian economy to fuel growth, Nehru, was restless about fast- tracking India's shift to industry – with a focus on steel and aerospace. But in pre-independence times, India's literacy was alarmingly low at about twelve percent and as a consequence, the country's economy paradigm was agrarian in principle. Do we see anything wrong with the practice of development economics in pre-independent India?

I do not choose to wade into the controversy, about whether or not Gandhi brought his religious convictions to bear on India's political and national ethos. In the opinion spectrum, some saw the partitioning of India as a British exit strategy, while others put the blame on politicians for India's political polarization which promoted a religious divide. Keep in mind, the Mahatma, a Hindu disciple, was assassinated by a Hindu zealot. Gandhi's wisdom, if anything, began the reform of the social ills that dominated Hindu society at the time - the caste system and *sati* being two of them.

It is perhaps more prudent, therefore, that critics realize it is not religion but the fundamental practice of religion that makes room for evil in the world.

In contrast, it would be important to examine how atheist thought and Marxist experiment in Stalin's Soviet Union, in Mao's China or in Pol Pot's Cambodia had brought on some of the most egregious crimes in human history.

The Communist Manifesto of Karl Marx promised a haven when men arrive at a world with no religion and called for a violent overthrow of the ruling class, the breaking down of social structures, property ownership and governance.

Rudolf Rummel, a political scientist observes in his piece "The Killing Machine that is Marxism" which appeared in *WorldNetDaily*: "Of all religions, secular and otherwise, that of Marxism has been by far the bloodiest... In practice, Marxism has meant bloody terrorism, deadly purges, lethal prison camps and murderous forced labor, fatal deportations, man-made famines, extrajudicial executions and fraudulent show trials, mass murder and genocide. In total, Marxist regimes murdered nearly 110 million people from 1917 to 1987... Marxism is more deadly than all the wars of the 20th century, including World Wars I and II, and the Korean and Vietnam Wars."[6]

Marxism may seemingly have professed noble goals and was designed and structured to inflict an assault on poverty, but as in any war, ordinary citizens were swallowed up in death. The net in that ideological battle was cast wide and trapped the clergy, capitalists, the landlords and intellectual elite.

As aforementioned, millions perished in those assaults on poverty and the ruling classes, that sought to hit the last nail on religion's coffin because Marx proclaimed religion to be the opiate of the people that stood in the way of grasping that God-free utopia. So atheism, despite its noble goals, strayed to become that deadly form of religion.

Apparently, Marx and Engels were impressed with Darwin's new revolutionary ideas about evolution. Conway Zirkle, Professor of Botany at the University of Pennsylvania, cites comments made in correspondence between Friedrich Engels and Karl Marx, in his book *Evolution, Marxian Biology, and the Social Scene*. Marx reportedly regarded Darwin's ideas of natural selection as the basis for the class struggle in history.[7]

The class struggle of the 20th century was a precursor of tyranny and genocide that reined in killing machines like Adolf Hitler's gas chambers that swallowed up millions of Jews. The two million Cambodians exterminated during Pol Pot's reign and the millions of Russian people dead under Stalin's rule paint that horrific picture quite fairly. The Soviet system of prison camps carried out thousands of executions.

In an address on the occasion of his acceptance, in London on May 10, 1983, of the Templeton Prize for Progress in Religion, Nobel Laureate Alexander Solzhenitsyn narrated that childhood story of what he was told about the great disaster that had befallen Russia: "That men had forgotten God and that is why all this had happened." This is an excerpt of that speech.

"More than half a century ago, while I was still a child, I recall hearing a number of older people offer the following explanation for the great disasters that had befallen Russia: 'Men have forgotten God; that's why all this has happened'."

He then goes on to say: "Since then I have spent well-nigh 50 years working on the history of our Revolution. In the process I have read hundreds of books, collected hundreds of personal testimonies, and have already contributed eight volumes of my own toward the effort of clearing away the rubble left by that upheaval.

"But if I were asked today to formulate as concisely as possible the main cause of the ruinous Revolution that swallowed up some 60 million of our people, I could not put it more accurately than to repeat: "Men have forgotten God; that's why all this has happened."[8]

CHAPTER 10

How religion-inspired work heals suffering
on the planet

After the Edict of Milan in 313, euphoria and change swept across Europe as persecutions of the Church were halted and monarchial societies broke down. The Christian story had begun shortly after the execution of Jesus with the rapid emergence of belief among his friends and followers that he rose from the dead. The first churches were variously organized, though very soon they began to assume a definite hierarchical form to sustain the wildfire spread of the news of the Gospels and the establishment of Christian communities throughout the world.[1]

Christianity swept across the West, bringing a new morality and influencing the very ethos of European societies in the span of the last 2000 years. The revolutionary teachings of Jesus Christ preached by the apostle Paul brought about a wind of change, halting infanticide, abolishing slavery, emancipating women, providing the tools to lift up the poor and marginalised, as well as providing for orphans, fostering justice and alleviating the sufferings of mankind.

Across Europe, Christian influences quickly saw the mushrooming of schools, orphanages and hospitals. It's influence on the social morality of nations and peoples was unprecedented in history and with a reformed morality came progress in the sphere of the arts across Europe. It is fair to say, unequivocally, Jesus of Nazareth shaped Western culture in the two millennia following his crucifixion.

A great part of that early evangelisation was led by the apostle Paul, who founded several churches in Asia Minor and Europe. He was both a Jew and a Roman citizen and brought that advantage to bear on his missionary work among both Jewish and Roman populations.

Prior to the Edict of Milan in the nascent years of Christianity, the church preached the sanctity of human life, sometimes to deaf ears, even as it opposed infanticide. But by the fourth century, when monarchial societies fell apart, social reform brought about change and legal sanctions against infanticide were introduced. Emperor Constantine, who issued the Edict of Milan, was a social reformer and in his time ordered speedy trials so that the innocence of those on trial would be assumed until conviction.

The Emperor Constantine turned the world upside down by recognizing Christianity instead of persecuting it like his predecessors. It meant freedom of worship and a church building boom. By the end of the 8th century, monasteries could reassemble villages with all their needs met in an enclosure dominated by the abbey church. Monasteries had found a stable character just when Europe was convulsed with wars and a breakdown of civilized life.[2]

Christianity also sought to reform and overthrow the enslavement of women, the other of the repressive social ills in European society at the time. Christian scriptures tell you that Jesus disregarded the Jewish anti-Samaritan prejudices and the misogynistic belief that a respectable man should not be seen speaking to a woman in public. When he met a Samaritan woman at Jacob's well, Jesus asked her for a drink. Shocked, she responded, "You are a Jew and I am a Samaritan woman. How can you ask me for a drink?" (John 4:9) Early Christianity despised misogyny. As a consequence, women were included in the life of the church and were set free from the shackles that bound them to Greco-Roman orthodoxy. In contrast to the abominable treatment of widows, the Christian approach to widows in the New Testament was a compassionate one. Jesus raised from the dead the son of the widow of Nain (Luke 7: 11-15), and at another time, hailed the widow who gave her only mite in her offering (Luke 21: 2-3)

The same exhortation by Paul, the apostle: "Neither slave nor free," worked its way down the centuries to put down slavery.

As history records, universal education came about with the Protestant Reformation in the sixteenth century with Luther and John Calvin defending education against radical reformers. The progress of science stepped up as scientists with Christian beliefs led the way, some of them being men like Leonardo da Vinci, Nicolaus Copernicus, Johannes Kepler, Galileo Galilei, Blaise Pascal, Michael Faraday, John Dalton and Louis Pasteur among so many others.

After the collapse of the Roman empire at the start of the fifth century, new foundations were needed if Christianity was to be a world force. Jerome, (born AD 342 and acknowledged as the most learned man of his day) produced a readable Bible, while Augustine of Hippo provided a theology that could survive the centuries. Augustine`s characteristic themes were the Fall (mankind sinning), the Atonement (Jesus Christ reconciling mankind with God), Grace (the application of God's love) and predestination (God's foreknowledge of people's response to his grace.)[3]

The years between 800 and 1200 saw a new pattern for Church and State. It began on Christmas Day AD 800 when Charlemagne was crowned in Rome by the Pope as the first Holy Roman Emperor.[4]

At the beginning of the 13th century, the life of Christian Europe was transformed by the invention of a new kind of dedicated preacher – the friar. Francis of Assisi attracted vast numbers simply by taking the Gospel literally. A formal rule prescribed poverty for the entire order – no money, no property.[5]

In modern times, the Church has acted with compassion in the face of violations of social justice at state levels and especially to redeem people from the brutality of communist regimes. Pope John Paul II's papacy had an indelible impact on the Church and the world with his influence in the fall of communism in Central and Eastern Europe. The film *"Liberating a Continent – John Paul II and the Fall of Communism*, which aired throughout the US and Canada in 2016, documents the spiritual revolution that led to the fall of the communist regime in Europe and the part that Karol Wojtyla, later John Paul II, played in the process.

Poland lost an estimated six million people during World War II, approximately 20 percent of its population. Then after the fall of the Nazi regime in 1945, Soviet communists took control of Poland and incorporated it into the Eastern bloc. John Paul II's first apostolic visit to his homeland as pope in 1979 "was the spark that ignited the peaceful protest movement that grew over the next decade leading to the eventual dissolution of the Eastern Bloc"[6]

A century ago as World War 1 raged in Europe, the US declared war on Germany and among the US servicemen sailing over to Europe were some 100,000 members of the Knights of Columbus including hundreds of clergy and war relief workers. The Knights' Committee on War Activities coordinated fundraisers and war relief efforts and the Order soon financed huts (recreation centers) in the US and around Europe. Donations poured in from Catholics and non-Catholics alike and funds finally "exceeded $14 million at a time when bread was seven cents a pound."[7]

Indeed, religion can still be a force for creating change in the world – there is evidence of this in the countless organizations that address poverty and marginalization and which reach out to incarcerated youth in penitentiaries with dedicated programs for reform that ultimately oversee the transition of past offenders into the mainstream of society.

Mother Theresa's work, first in the slums of Calcutta, then through the Missionaries of Charity she founded in 1950, may have touched millions of lives. Her missions were spread across 133 countries, managing homes for people dying of HIV/AIDS, leprosy and tuberculosis; soup kitchens; dispensaries and mobile clinics; orphanages, and schools.[8] Like Teresa's Missionaries of Charity, the Christian organization, Women of Hope International works with war victims in Sierra Leone.

Several Jewish organizations, especially in the United States are focussed on fighting social justice and human rights issues.

T'ruah brings a rabbinic voice and the power of the Jewish community to protecting and advancing human rights in North America, Israel, and the occupied Palestinian territories. It does this by training and mobilizing a network of 2,000 rabbis and cantors, together with their communities, to bring Jewish values to life through strategic and meaningful action. It empowers synagogues and other communities to protect immigrants and refugees through Mikdash: The Jewish Sanctuary Network. It mobilizes rabbis and their communities to support a better future for both Israelis and Palestinians by ending the occupation and establishing a two-state solution. It organizes rabbis and their communities to support the only proven solution to slavery in U.S. agriculture, through partnership with the Coalition of Immokalee Workers and the Worker-Driven Social Responsibility Network. It advocates for the rights of minority communities in Israel, including African asylum seekers and Palestinian and Bedouin citizens. It is working to end mass incarceration in the United States, as a step toward dismantling long-term systemic racism. It is organizing rabbis to act as a moral voice against torture, including the ongoing practice of solitary confinement in U.S. prisons.[9]

The World Council of Churches has initiated a program called *Thursdays in Black* as a campaign to end violence against women. The program focuses on ways that individuals can challenge attitudes that cause rape and violence, on a personal and public level. It provides an opportunity for people to become part of a worldwide movement which enables the despair, pain and anger about rape and other forms of violence to be transformed into political action.[10]

Likewise there are hundreds of other Christian groups dedicated to effecting change in our world, bringing hope to the marginalised and social justice to our societies. Those include organizations like *Nuns On the Bus* who work across the United States of America for immigration reform, bridging the divide, income equality and other social injustice issues; *Ten Thousand Homes*, a non-profit organization building strength, courage, stability, and a future for the most vulnerable of the developing world.

In much the same way, Bahá'i, Jewish, Muslim, Sikh, Hindu and other faith groups as well can be seen around the world standing together to effect change: the AVODAH Jewish Service Corps works on issues like immigration, education, homelessness and criminal justice; the Ahmadiyya Muslim Youth Association is involved in works of charity - organizing blood drives, food drives, clothes drives, highway cleanups and adopt-a-family services to provide support to at-risk families around the United States; Khalsa Aid is a Sikh humanitarian organization that sends relief to disaster regions; Islamic Relief USA is an international aid organization providing relief and development and working to alleviate poverty.

The elimination of the extremes of wealth and poverty is one of the spiritual principles enunciated by Bahá'u'lláh, the founder of the Baha'i faith – a principle essential to the foundation of "a world economy characterized by justice."

At the 2016 Spiritual Diversity Conference I hosted in Canada, Dr. Ann Boyles, Editor of *The Bahá'i World*, an international record of the activities and thought of the Bahá'í international community, shared some of those views with conference delegates to demonstrate how the Bahá'í grassroots initiatives have empowered people to become the agents of their own and their community's social and spiritual transformation.

Dr. Boyles talked about the Bahá'í experience in Vanuatu, a nation with a population of some 250,000 people, located in the South Pacific Ocean and where, on March 14, 2015, the tropical cyclone Pam passed directly through, bringing in its wake, devastation in the village of Namasmetene on the Island of Tanna. "But unfazed by the misfortune, Bahá'í youth reconstructed shelters and led villagers back towards their destroyed gardens urging their elders to replant what had been damaged and salvage what they could from damage by the sun," she said. "The replanting was a way to ensure that in three months' time, all families in the village would have enough food to survive."

Dr. Boyles said that for some twenty years, since 1996, the Bahá'í community of Vanuatu has been engaged in a systematic effort to build capacity with anyone interested and willing to join it in a collaborative learning process. "There are classes that further the spiritual education of the youngest participants, aged approximately six to eleven years. They centre on the building of character, inculcating virtues such as kindness, generosity and laying the foundation of a moral structure that will be built throughout the individual's entire life," she said.

"The youth of Vanuatu, who have been studying and reflecting about the coherence between their own spiritual development and the transformation of the communities in which they live, have become aware that through their actions, they have the power to affect their environment for the better, and they have developed the skills, capacities and attitudes that impel them towards action," Dr. Boyle told conference delegates.

"Their intimate knowledge of the situation on the ground, their ability to collect statistics, plan, consult, reflect, write reports, and act systematically—all were beneficial to the relief effort in the two weeks following the cyclone."

She said the experience of Vanuatu is dramatic, but the three-stage educational process used there, is part of a global grassroots education system which has the power to equip participants to contribute to the building of a truly prosperous world civilization. It is a process that is unfolding, she notes, in every corner of the world, in rural settings, small villages, towns, large urban centres; in simple huts or under shady trees, in community centres and comfortable homes.

"I am not saying that it is easy," Dr. Boyles said. "It has provided many challenges to the thousands and thousands of participating communities. But undeniably, the capacity to effect change is emerging 'as the protagonists of social change learn to apply with increasing effectiveness, elements of Bahá'u'lláh's Revelation, together with the contents and methods of science, to their social reality'."

The Aga Khan Development Network (AKDN) is an endeavour of the Ismaili Imamat to realise the social conscience of Islam through institutional action. It brings together institutions and programs whose combined mandate is to relieve society of ignorance, disease and deprivation without regard to the faiths or national origins of people whom they serve. Its primary areas of concern are the poorest regions of Asia and Africa and the institutions derive their impetus from the ethics of Islam which bridge the two realms of the faith: din and dunya, the spiritual and the material.

The AKDN and its agencies are not religious organisations, although its work is underpinned by the ethical principles of Islam – particularly consultation, solidarity with those less fortunate, self-reliance and human dignity.

It currently operates more than a thousand programs and institutions – many of which date back over sixty years, and some over a hundred. It employs approximately 80,000 people, the majority of whom are based in developing countries. Its annual budget for non-profit development work is approximately US$950 million. [11]

The network focuses, in part, on rural development and assists in the struggle against hunger, disease, ignorance and social exclusion. It is largely a field-based organisation with program units in at least thirty countries including Afghanistan, Bangladesh, Egypt, India, Kenya, the Kyrgyz Republic, Madagascar, Mali, Mozambique, Pakistan, Portugal, Russia, Syria, Tajikistan, Tanzania, Uganda and several more, with resource mobilisation offices in Canada, the United Kingdom and the United States.

AKDN's rural support program in India, alone, reaches more than one million beneficiaries in nearly 1,900 villages in Gujarat, Madhya Pradesh and Bihar. It offers a range of financial services from community-based savings groups to corporate banking and life insurance. These services serve at least 17 million people on the planet every year.

But aside from rural development, AKF's remit is much larger. In Eastern Africa, for example, hospitals and clinics of the Aga Khan Health Services (AKHS) and the Aga Khan University (AKU) provide a network of healthcare facilities that range from rural clinics to a major teaching hospital in Nairobi. AKU also runs medical and nursing degree programs in the region to build human resources. In addition to the expansion of the medical facilities in Nairobi, AKU plans the construction of a Faculty of Arts and Sciences in Arusha, Tanzania. The Aga Khan Academies, which aim to educate a new generation of leaders for Africa, began operating its first school in Mombasa, Kenya in 2003. Each academy is a resource centre for the professional development of teachers in their area.

The project companies of the Aga Khan Fund for Economic Development (AKFED) play a major economic role that supports the social projects. Frigoken, for example, works with 75,000 small-holder farmers to process green beans for the European market. The Nation Group, a major component of Eastern Africa's civil society since it was launched at independence, publishes newspapers and broadcasts radio and television. The US$900 million Bujagali hydroelectric project, Uganda's first private hydroelectric power project, produces nearly 50 percent of the country's electricity. The Serena Hotels, another AKFED project company that operates 24 hotel properties in the region, has been an important innovator in culturally and environmentally sensitive tourism. Other project companies operate in key industries such as agricultural packaging, finance, aviation and pharmaceuticals. The Aga Khan Trust for Culture (AKTC), the cultural agency of the Network, focuses on culture as a means to leverage cultural assets in order to spur economic growth.

The aim of this integrated effort is to introduce a range of disciplines and a variety of catalysts that, in combination, help spark a broad advance of economic, cultural and social development and improvements in the quality of life."

Likewise, there are thousands of other development centres across the world managed by faith organizations that seek to lift marginalized communities that struggle on account of poverty and illiteracy – the principal causes for the disruption of peace in our world. This chapter, unfortunately, cannot adequately cover them all.

CHAPTER 11

Is God really relevant today?

"God is not like a 'one-plus-one-equals-two' thing"
Christopher Weppner *

Just moments after the twin towers in New York were hit by planes, the question on the streets was "Where is God?" Well, is God relevant today? That response depends on who you are talking to.

She could be someone who has just lost her only child in a car accident, is broken and shattered and is now desperately crying out for a response to "Where is God?" On the other hand, he may be someone who believes that there is no God and that the question "Where is God?" is superfluous.

If you are talking to the former, you grieve with her. Like the Christian evangelist Billy Graham, who spoke to crowds three days after the 9/11 tragedy, confess to her that you do not know the answer, but that the Christian narrative on suffering and death does not end with the cross, for Easter points beyond the tragedy of the cross to the empty tomb, as the evangelist had observed. It tells us that there is hope for eternal life.

At the end of July 2017, tragedy struck our family like a rock hurled in the face and all of us were engulfed in utter gloom. My niece's eldest son, barely 20, was called to heaven in a flash. In a private moment I spoke to his mom. Sobbing, she said to me: "He was God's child. He loaned the child to me and now He has taken him home. His will be done." There is grandeur in that view.

Dr. Sarfati observes: "The big picture is that Adam's sin is the reason for all the death in the world. A consistent biblical answer points out that death is an intruder, so it is not part of God's original creation, but is ultimately due to man's sin."[1]

But if you're speaking to someone who believes that God is a figment of the imagination, then that response is very different. He would probably be satisfied with Darwin's view: "In looking at Nature, it is most necessary to keep the foregoing considerations always in mind—never to forget that every single organic being around us may be said to be striving to the utmost to increase in numbers; that each lives by a struggle at some period of its life; that heavy destruction inevitably falls either on the young or old, during each generation or at recurrent intervals."[2]

God, anyway, is absolutely relevant today. That is premised despite the scientific assumption that we are a bag of atoms that have evolved from random reactions of chemicals around the universe. This may sound like nasty sarcasm. But although one may try hard as one can, it is challenging to stomach the point of view that the mystery of the human spirit, the complexity of human behaviour, the factors priming reason, emotion or imagination have come together by chance arrangements of amino acids.

If science has not come up with the answers to 'why do we have a universe instead of nothing at all,' if science cannot tell us why we are here and what happens to us after death, God is absolutely relevant today.

His relevance in the world would never be dubious if the ethos of our global societies reflected a glowing spirituality: people working for the uplift of the poor, the emancipation of women, compassion for the despairing, the removal of race barriers and social injustice. Is that not, anyway, what a godly world would seek to do?

Imagine a world where people love their enemies, do good to those who harm them. Imagine a world that is poor in spirit, that hungers and thirsts after righteousness, a world that is merciful, pure of heart. Imagine a world of peacemakers. If you can imagine a world like that, you do not have to imagine a world without religion.

The struggle against poverty and human suffering is at the heart of some of our problems in the world today. Fighting that struggle together can become a clarion call to faith groups seeking to unshackle the marginalised from their binding chains. Since poverty constitutes a big part of human suffering, its alleviation can become the prime driving force for interfaith collaboration in human development. God is witnessed in a spiritual haven.

Pope Francis has been speaking of the need for religious leaders to come together in dialogue in his recent trips to Egypt, Turkey, Sri Lanka and elsewhere and faith groups must seize this moment. On November 3, 2016, speaking to representatives of different religions at Clementine Hall, he despaired of the fact that acts of violence and conflict are a daily occurrence and called for religious freedom and the fostering of peaceful encounter among believers.

Solzhenitsyn, as noted in the previous chapter, came to a conclusion after 50 years of work on his country's history, gleaning through hundreds of books and personal testimonies, that the cause for the egregious revolution that swallowed up 60 million people in the Soviet Union was simply because "Men have forgotten God." That's the mistake in history that we cannot afford to repeat. If His relevance must be witnessed, people of faith must reflect His compassion for the poor, His mercy, His love of mankind, His sense of justice and exercise one's free will to build a world that challenges the spiritual being within us. -

Sayed Dr. Moustaffa al-Qazwini, speaking at the third Spiritual Diversity Conference, in Halifax, October 2016, told delegates: "Islam advocates justice, peace, righteousness. So, whoever is associated with these principles is respected in Islam. We subscribe to one family, one club, to one order and that is humanity. We therefore must get together for one cause and should not be divided. It is thus important that we forge relationships and foster friendship. Interfaith and intra-faith relations help to dispel misconceptions."

Shastri Robert Gailey of the Halifax Shambhala Centre, speaking on *The Spiritual Dimension of Human Existence as the Basis for Peaceful Co-existence*, at the same conference, told delegates that peaceful coexistence requires a rousing of the human spirit that can unite a visionary approach that touches the sublime aspects of experience (the spiritual) with the practicalities of the earth on which we live. "In Shambhala, we have shorthand for this vision; we call it 'joining heaven, earth and humanity.' In human life, conflict is inevitable and, in fact, is not necessarily bad. A strong and successful society must be able to accommodate and resolve human conflict without physical or psychological violence."

"This brings us back to the individual," he said. "As leaders and citizens, our primary social responsibility is to understand and conquer the seeds of self-centeredness in ourselves and others so that our innate virtue can shine forth without obstruction. Then, naturally our words and deeds that offer kindness and insight will bring a more peaceful and prosperous world."

Father Raymond J. de Souza is a Roman Catholic priest of the Archdiocese of Kingston, Ontario, where he serves as chaplain for Newman House, the Catholic chaplaincy at Queen's University. He is also a columnist of the *National Post* in Canada. Speaking at the Spiritual Diversity Conference in Halifax in 2011 on *How Can We Respond to the Challenges presented by Religious Diversity in Canada*, he addressed five dimensions to the perspective:

First, religion has been a growing factor in global public life in the late 20th and early 21st century. This has an impact on Canadian public life as well, partly through immigration and partly through more assertive religious identity. Second, religious liberty is the first liberty and an essential public one, so any liberal democratic society has to make room for the religious in public life. Third, Canadian multiculturalism must take into account religious identity and practice, for culture at its heart is religious. Fourth, the diversity question is not about whether there is enough room for different religions, but whether there is room for religion at all. The battle as it were, is not between religions but between the aggressively secular and the religious. Fifth, the danger is this: the growth of secular fundamentalism in public life can be successful in marginalizing religious voices, but at the risk of radicalizing.

"We have seen this in some of the most secular nations in Europe," he says. "Their multicultural projects have been officially declared failures because large numbers of immigrants have declared themselves uninterested in becoming secular hedonists, and therefore built parallel societies in which radicalism has flourished." He was making the point that precisely by denying any role for religion in public life, it has been driven to the margins, where it has developed precisely the pathologies one expects to find at the margins. He concluded saying: "Our Canadian experience is not this. It's our challenge of diversity and remains our contribution toward a just and peaceful society."

God is revealed either mystically or through holy scripture and the witnessing experience of his relevance might come from those who translate His compassion, His love, His sense of justice on the ground in communities across the planet. God is seen in the goodness of humanity.

On the Mount of Olives, Jesus sat his disciples down and talked to them in parables – of trouble and persecution, the coming of the Son of Man, and of the Final Judgement.

"When the Son of Man comes in his glory, and all the angels with him, then he will sit on his glorious throne. Before him will be gathered all the nations, and he will separate people one from another as a shepherd separates the sheep from the goats. And he will place the sheep on his right, but the goats on the left. Then the King will say to those on his right, 'Come, you who are blessed by my Father, inherit the kingdom prepared for you from the foundation of the world. For I was hungry and you gave me food, I was thirsty and you gave me drink, I was a stranger and you welcomed me, I was naked and you clothed me, I was sick and you visited me, I was in prison and you came to me.' Then the righteous will answer him, saying, 'Lord, when did we see you hungry and feed you, or thirsty and give you drink? And when did we see you a stranger and welcome you, or naked and clothe you? And when did we see you sick or in prison and visit you?' And the King will answer them, 'Truly, I say to you, as you did it to one of the least of these my brothers, you did it to me.' (Matthew 25: 31-40)

In a troubled world, mankind represents the hands and feet of the Lord. It's important that Christians help build an egalitarian world structured on the compassion and morality proclaimed in the *Sermon on the Mount*. In so doing, we shall reach out to millions of people caught up in the struggle for survival. Then those that have eyes shall witness, the goodness of Creation shall light the way forward and those who have never felt the mystical touch of the Creator, will come face to face with Him.

Hawking's dream of a Theory of Everything is now utopic, as discussed in an earlier chapter, and so it's probably appropriate at this time to reconcile with the fact that science may never know the mind of God. Instead, perhaps you and I reflecting in awe on the wonders of His universe and of His holy omnipresence may grasp that mystical moment and get a glimpse of that sacred mind, when we seek it in complete humility.

God will be relevant to the universe for as long as the set of laws that govern it must prevail; the physical constants that make the planet hospitable to life must stay tuned in their goldilocks zones; the sun must light up the firmament and day must follow night, and the earth must be made warm so that we may bask in it; the awesome seas must be the habitat of fish and crustaceans, the seagulls must glide across them; the rain must fall gently upon our fields, so that it grows our crops, and brings fruit to our lands and the bread of life to sustain us all; the rivers and lakes must flow in peaceful serenity with abundant water to quench our thirst.

He will be relevant to mankind for as long as a child must be born to bring joy to a mother, so that love will prevail and become ubiquitous, bringing serenity to the soul, compassion for the marginalised and a sense of social justice for all. Man will witness His presence for as long as the moral law stands between good and evil, until all of mankind can see the truth and appreciate the grandeur of His creation and the heavens and earth shall become one. God will be relevant until death – the last enemy (1 Corinthians 15:26) has been conquered.

If then, God is the first cause, any question about His relevance should stop there.

---

* Christopher Weppner is a seven year old lad, who made this observation in a conversation with the family at the dinner table sometime ago

ADDENDUM

A common ground in world religions

A selection of presentations by faith leaders made at the spiritual diversity conferences hosted in Halifax in 2011, 2013 and 2016.

There is a sense among people of faith that religion and interfaith conversations can become the critical solution to today's grave problems. Hate, intolerance, tyranny and violence have no place in a world that's looking to create for itself peaceful societies. But as people of different faiths take up residence in the West – and that will happen because immigration spurs economic growth – the challenge of accommodating religious diversity, especially within the framework of secular governance gets more pointed. That nations are struggling with ways to accommodate religious diversity is witnessed at large. In Canada, for example, it is witnessed in the very public debates, some years ago, over the funding of religious schools, the call for faith-based arbitration or the introduction of Muslim Sharia law into the country's penal code, the lobbying by a section of Ontario's Hindus for a waterway designated for traditional burial rituals and a call for the establishment of a commission in Quebec looking into reasonable accommodation of diverse cultural practices focused on religious diversity.

So between 2011 and 2016, I convened three Spiritual Diversity Conferences in Halifax that saw delegates and religious scholars converge on the city from across North America to address the challenges of our time – the injustices within our global society, the social inequality, the racial prejudice, moral and ethical issues that divide us as a people.

These conferences were designed to seek commonalities as well as acknowledge differences and make a commitment to engage in civil discourse. The hope was to promote greater interfaith understanding with people affirming a respect for the religious beliefs of others, promoting egalitarianism and affirming respect at the same time for Canada's core democratic values.

This far, Canada has confronted these challenges excellently. But as the pluralism patina matures, the challenge will be greater. I say greater because I believe public opinion surveys reveal that relations between faith communities and secular Canadians are now a very important preoccupation. There is a significant demographic change in the country – characterized by considerable growth in the percentage of Canadians who are not Christian as well as an increase in Canadians reporting no religion. There is already evidence of an exponential growth in religions from South and East Asia, Africa and the Middle East.

At the other end of the spectrum, September 11 and its subsequent war on terror raised many questions about what triggered that egregious cataclysm and how our societies can work for a paradigm shift from the inevitable clash of civilizations to a dialogue of civilizations.

It's very obvious that these new challenges to western societies have emerged as the need to grow economies have pushed governments to look for steady growth in their populations as well as production skills through immigration. But the hundreds of thousands of newcomers that are headed to countries in the West every year are not going to leave their religion at the door and come in. That is because culture at its root is religious. How then, do we accommodate religious diversity in a secular framework of governance?

If you look closely at what is triggering violence across the world – you see hatred, bigotry and xenophobia raising its ugly ahead. So, is religion the cause of it all or does religion have a role to play in transforming a violent world into a peaceful one? Where does hatred lie? Can religion help? On the other hand, do world religions have a perspective on human rights?

Looking inward as Canadians, for example, we may have to ask the question, does the founding population see Muslims as different from themselves? Can we bring spirituality into the workplace and in everyday life? How do ethnic communities identify with their faith traditions in Canada or anywhere else where migrants take up residence?

Finally, keep in mind, that the battle, as it were, is not between religions but between the aggressively secular and the religious. In his presentation at the first Spiritual Diversity Conference hosted in Halifax in 2011, Fr. Raymond de Souza, made the point that the growth of secular fundamentalism in public life can be successful in marginalizing religious voices, but at the risk of radicalization.

Excerpts from presentations made at these conferences and reproduced in this final chapter will provide a window on the spiritual perspectives of the major faith groups around the world and share the conversations that were brought to the table in the effort to seek solutions to the challenges of our time. These presentations have a Canadian perspective.

A Jewish Perspective

Rabbi Ari Isenberg, formerly Rabbi at the Shaar Shalom Synagogue in Halifax, speaks to conference delegates on *Religion, Spirituality and Humanism – The Challenge from Youth* at the Spiritual Diversity Conference, Halifax, Canada, October 2013

In researching my topic today, I decided to speak with some Jewish teenagers and university students. One of the individuals I spoke to graduated with a bachelor's degree two years ago and is now out in the work force. She is Jewish and defines herself as secular, though fairly cultural; but not at all religious. I asked her to describe a typical daily routine for me. This was her response:

"I wake up and do a 10-minute mind-soul-body meditative grounding exercise. I then water my plants, feed my cat, make breakfast and head out for a quick run. I'm training for a 10k to raise money for a charitable foundation. I then go to my office." Her office, by the way, is part of a non-profit organization that seeks to find intermediary employment for opera singers who are between roles.

Now, she defines herself as secular. And yet, it would seem, on the surface, that this young woman is fervently religious and lives a life according to profound and rich religious precepts and beliefs. After all, she wakes up and meditates: in Judaism, we call that a form of prayer – *kavanah*. Spontaneous soul-directing prayer. It is a Jewish commandment.

She then feeds her animals, her plants, and nourishes her own body – all of this taking after the Matriarch Rebeccah. When Abraham's servant heads out to find a wife for his son Isaac, he encounters Rebeccah and becomes impressed by her because of her desire to ensure that his animal and he have enough to drink and eat.

She then goes for a run, taking care of her body – another Jewish principle. And what's she training for? A fundraiser marathon – in Hebrew, we call that *tzedakah*, a foundational tenet of our tradition. Finally, she goes to work – also a Jewish commandment. The Hebrew dictum is *"ein Torah bli kemach"* – there is no Torah without labour. That means, if all you wish to do is sit around all day and study scripture, who's going to put food on the table? You must go out and provide for yourself. Balance!

I suspect this example in my tradition probably resonates for you and recalls for you examples in your own faith communities. These are young people who are filling their days with noble, sacred, inherently religious acts, and yet do not themselves associate those acts as being in any way religiously driven. What causes this disconnect? How might we recapture the basic religious actions and rituals in our daily lives and see them for what they inherently are: rooted in religious tradition?

In Judaism, our entire system of religious actions and behaviours is categorized as fulfilling Jewish *Mitzvot*. A *mitzvah* can be anything from opening the door for an elder to fasting on Yom Kippur to praying each day, and so on. Mitzvah is a word not easily defined, but we often define it as a commandment.

Now let me ask you to think for a quick moment: What motivates someone to obey a commandment, a law? One of my teachers, Rabbi Brad Artson, offers one motivation: fear. In his words, this is an ancient pedigree, but in order for fear to work, you have to believe it. So, if you really think that the Creator of the universe watching you eat the pork chop will make your spouse leave you or your boss fire you; if you really believe that, then that's a strong motivator to not have that pork chop.

The problem with this position is that goodness is not always rewarded; evil is not always punished. It seems there are random relationships between moral decency and outcome. Expecting the universe to treat you well because you're good is like expecting the bull not to charge because you're vegetarian (Kuschner). If it's true among people, it's even more true in the universe. Bad things aren't dished out as punishments. They just happen.

So believing in doing commandments out of fear of God isn't a tenable position because the moment something bad happens in your life, you might then come to a realization that all of these commandments didn't bring you what you hoped for, so you'll now just do away with them all. The flipside of that theology: I don't think God cares what I put in my mouth, and I don't think God cares if I read from a prayer book. If you think that the only reason to obey commandments is because there's some powerful guy who's going to punish you and if you don't believe that, then there's no point doing them.

Most North American Jews bounce back and forth between those two, binary, opposite, polar theologies. So we need a new understanding of commandment and why we do them.

Anita Diamant discovered that, while in Hebrew, Mitzvah means commandment/law, in Aramaic, the root *tzaveh* means to join, to bring together... moments of connection, moments of belonging. We believe, if anything, that the divine is our recognition of something bigger than ourselves – loved ones, ancestors, community, history, culture, future, universe, all living things. If we start to see *mitzvah* as our ability to connect with others, with community, we might be more inclined to label our daily actions as *mitzvot*. Fulfilling *Mitzvot* is like the ultimate social media app! And why do them? The answer is found right in the middle of the Torah – right in the center of the book of Leviticus... "You Shall Be Holy, for I, your God, am Holy." We are commanded to be holy people. I would like to assert that achieving holiness is about turning our ordinary moments into something greater, something more meaningful - to transform the mundane or regular moments of our lives into a series of spiritually profound, meaningful, and holy occasions.

There is no need to do away with your secular lifestyle; simply reposition your outlook. Infuse those ordinary moments with enhanced spirituality. I would like to argue that an active secular life and a deeply profound holy and religious life are not mutually exclusive. They can be expressed concurrently and, often are, when seen in proper perspective.

I started this morning with the anecdote of a college graduate whose life is filled with *mitzvot,* with moments of religious connection, with moments infusing the ordinary with holiness and significance, yet she herself doesn't see it that way, with that perspective. I would like to leave you with another anecdote. It's about a 21-year-old Jewish university student and it takes place on a Saturday night at pizza corner – so brace yourself.

She was out, drinking a few martinis, laughing, dancing, maybe even meeting someone there and getting a phone number to arrange for a coffee date. It was a wonderful night, but it's now 2:00 am and they're all on their way home. On their way, they decide to stop at Pizza Corner for a slice of pizza. This young lady notices that they only have pepperoni pizza left. She asks how long it would take to make a veggie pizza. The pizza guy says that he can make a vegetarian pizza, but it will take eight minutes. This girl chooses to wait there for eight minutes, rather than eat the pepperoni pizza.

Think about it— it's 2:00 am, the night was about socializing, drinking, dancing, and now a decision that, ultimately, stems all the way back to the Torah… a decision influenced by Jewish law. What a powerful moment that is.

If we can communicate to our youth that secular and religious moments can be concurrent, can enhance each other, that we can actually feel augmented by the combination of both, that we can feel an enhanced sense of connection with our families, our communities, humanity, perhaps we'll be more successful at helping them live their lives through that lens.

A Christian Perspective

Rev. Fr. Owen Connolly, Assistant Pastor at a church in Halifax speaks briefly
on the whole notion of *Mystery: Why Is It So Challenging For Westerners?*
He shares some thoughts, as well, on the *Sermon on the Mount* at the
Spiritual Diversity Conference, Halifax, Canada, October 2016

Fr. Karl Rahner, a German Jesuit and one of the most influential theologians in the twentieth century, in Roman Catholic tradition, said sometime before his death: "The only Christians who will survive in the post-modern world, will be those who are mystics." At the time, I don't think the statement resonated with the Catholic world, in the same way as it does today. For as time goes on and we go deeper and deeper into the twenty first century, many are beginning to realize just how important this insight should be for us. Why is it so challenging for Westerners?

I believe it is so challenging because we are so uncomfortable with the whole notion of mystery. We are cerebral people, in many ways dualistic and so if we are not able to explain an event, through our highly technical minds, then we tend to dismiss it.

We have great difficulty simply standing before the mystery and when we are forced to confront the whole mystery of life, we are unable, like Moses, to just take off our shoes and let the mystery wash over us. And as the mystery washes over us, it tends to unfold before us. But this involves living from our hearts and not from our heads. Yet we teach that the way in which we come to faith is by listening with our ears, believing in our hearts and professing with our lips. It's the heart that we have trouble with.

The way we enter into a mystery is not through study or research, but rather through prayer – contemplative prayer. Mystical prayer was not practiced in our schools but was rather taught as a subject. So we came to know about mystical prayer but had not really practiced it in our lives. However, in the middle of the twentieth century came along a man, whose name was Thomas Merton and who once again introduced us to the practice of contemplation. He showed us that contemplation was not only an important part of our prayer, but rather contemplation was the way the early church fathers prayed. Men like Ignatius of Antioch, Cyprian and Augustine were great contemplatives, men of deep prayer.

However, at the end of the fourth century, history tells us things changed significantly, when Christianity became the official religion of the empire. Now the Church moved in a very different direction moving from a minority to a majority. This changed our outlook on life. Instead of living out of our poverty we began to be a part of the majority and in many ways took on the ways of the world. Mystical theology was now being threatened. However, in response to this movement, holy men and women went off to the Egyptian desert to pray in the 3rd and 4th century. They were not necessarily great scholars, but rather they were people of deep prayer. People who dedicated themselves to prayer, work and contemplation and at the door of each of these monasteries one would discover a strong ministry for the poor. It was a great outreach.

Thomas Merton in the 20th century was the first to observe that these people were like Zen masters. Among them were great theologians including a learned Greek by the name Vanquis Apontos who said: A theologian is one who prays and one who prays is a theologian. It's not in study but rather in prayer that we come to know about God personally.

With the advent of the Second Vatican Council in 1961, the Fathers of the Council paid great tribute to the enormous contribution of Eastern Christianity when they said: "Moreover in the East are to be found the riches of those spiritual traditions to which monasticism gives special expression. From the glorious days of the early holy Fathers, there flourished in the east that monastic spirituality which later flowed over into the western world and then provided a source from which Latin monastic life took its rise and has drawn much fresh vigour ever since.

Therefore, Catholics are strongly urged to avail themselves of these spiritual riches of the Eastern Fathers which lift up the whole person to the contemplation of the divine mysteries.

Mysticism is about relationships – relationship with our God, relationship with one another. It is interesting that an ancient mystic once said: "If we are praying in a room and cannot hear the cry of a child in the room next door, our prayer is not authentic."

Perhaps the two best mystics in the 20th century in the Roman Catholic tradition are Mother Teresa and Jean Vanier. It is important to note that these two people, giants of people, are deeply spiritual people who through different but similar experience from both sides of the world hear the word of God being directly spoken in their hearts and they leave their secure lives and decide to follow Jesus in poverty, simplicity and obedience to God's will.

How do they do this? In very simple ways: Mother Teresa gathered a few volunteers around her to respond to the needs of people in the streets of Calcutta who were virtually dying in the streets, unattended. She simply went out and began to comfort them by bringing them into a shelter, attending to their basic needs for bathing, food, comfort and companionship. Someone asked her how she was going to do this. She said simply, "one person at a time."

Jean Vanier on the other hand, heard the call of God when he was teaching philosophy at the University of Toronto and the call was simply to go out and minister to the needs of people with mental disabilities, especially those with down syndrome. He went out and invited two of them to live with him. There he planned to provide a home environment for them – very warm, simple, truly gospel-based, but unexpectedly there arose from that little home a movement that spread to many countries in the world.

What inspired these two mystics to move out? It was simply their fascination with the *Sermon on the Mount*. It is Jesus' teaching – not just a teaching that we have become familiar with, but a teaching we are called to put into practice in everyday life. It is the basic teaching of the Gospel which should be for Catholics what the Commandments are to the Hebrew people. Just as Moses ascended to the mountain and received the guidelines for life, so did Jesus ascend to the mountain and delivered to those who were to become his disciples, the guidelines for Christian living. Those that take these words and apply them in their lives are called Christian. But the real meaning of the term is to be a Christ bearer – to bear the teachings and the life of Christ in our lives.

The teachings are intended for all people of good will and I was really struck some many years ago reading Mahatma Gandhi's philosophy of non-violence and learning that he based his teachings on the *Sermon on the Mount*. Gandhi was, of course, a devout Hindu and a great admirer of Jesus. He knew the teachings of Jesus more than most Christians of his era. This was also the inspiration for people like Desmond Tutu and Martin Luther King.

So let's listen to the words of the *Sermon on the Mount* from Matthew's gospel:

"When he saw the crowds, he went up to the mountain and after he sat down, his disciples came. He began to teach them saying:

Blessed are the poor in spirit, for theirs is the kingdom of heaven. Blessed are they who mourn, for they will be comforted. Blessed are the meek, for they will inherit the land. Blessed are they who hunger and thirst for righteousness, for they will be satisfied. Blessed are the merciful, for they will be shown mercy. Blessed are the clean in heart, for they will see God. Blessed are the peacemakers, for they will be called children of God. Blessed are they who are persecuted for the sake of righteousness, for theirs is the kingdom of heaven

So, for us as Christians, the *Sermon on the Mount* in Matthew's gospel is what we are called to live by. One of our great challenges with the Christian church is that we have what I call a power outage. We teach and believe that the parabola of transformation of life is the passion and death of our Lord Jesus Christ. There are far too many Christians in the world today who want to come to the resurrection without going through the passion and death. Christianity is not a label that we wear but a life that we live.

An Islamic Perspective

Dr. Jamal Badawi, North America's respected scholar on Islam, addresses conference delegates on the topic *September 11 and the Future of World Peace* at the Spiritual Diversity Conference hosted in Halifax, Canada, October 2011. He lays bare some of the essential tenets and decrees of Islam and its position on human brotherhood, universal peaceful coexistence, peaceful dialogue and some misinterpretations. These are excerpts which explain the Qur'anic Foundations of World Peace

In religious history, there have been some elements within various faith communities who see relationship with other communities in terms of conflict, dominance and antagonism. Some have been able to use, or more correctly, abuse revealed or sacred texts to justify wars, massacres and even genocides. It is sad to note that these attitudes continue in our "civilized" world. There is hope, however, through religious leaders like those present here, to speak up and respond to the extremist fringes within your own faith communities. An authentic response may include the exposition and articulation of the forgotten or ignored positive values and teachings that are opposed to extremist misrepresentation of your faiths. The response, I believe, should include correction of common misinterpretations of certain passages in your faith traditions.

May I humbly share with you what I tried to do within my own faith community both before and after 9/11. This exposition is meant to give a practical example of my proposal.

On World Peace And Justice: It should be noted from the beginning that the very term Islam implies that peace is the basis and the norm of Muslim/Non-Muslim relations. Islam is derived from the Arabic root [S-L-M] whose generic meaning includes the concepts —peace and submission. From a spiritual perspective, Islam may be defined as attaining peace through submission to Allah or the state of peace in submission to Allah. References in the Qur'an and *Hadeeth* reveal that this concept of peace embraces peace with God, inner peace as a result of that relationship with God, peace with humans, peace with the animal world, peace with vegetation and peace with the ecological order.

On Faith In The One Universal God: [Allah in Arabic]: Islam is founded on the belief that there is only one God, who is the universal Creator, Sustainer and Cherisher of all. Being the sole creator of all humankind precludes any notion of multiple, competing creators, each marshalling his creation against the other gods and their creation. Allah is One and is impartial toward His creation. He

107

provides for all, including those who reject faith in Him, or even those who defy Him. He cares for the well being of all and gives them ample opportunity to repent to Him and end the state of separateness suffered by those who reject Him or are unmindful of Him. This belief implies that all humans are equal before Allah in terms of their humanity, irrespective of their particular beliefs.

On Unity And Universality Of The Core Teachings Of All Prophets: That core message is peace in submission to Allah; literally Islam. According to the Qur'an, a Muslim must accept, revere and believe in all the prophets of Allah, without discrimination. They all represent one brotherhood of faith extending vertically to include many generations and horizontally to embrace all humanity. In the Qur'an we read: we [Muslims] make no distinction between any of His messengers [i.e. God's messengers] 2:285. We read also: Behold, We have revealed to you [O Muhammad] as We revealed to Noah and all the prophets after him... 4: 163. Still in another verse we read: In matters of faith, He [God] has ordained for you that which He had enjoined upon Abraham, Moses and Jesus: steadfastly uphold the [true] faith and make no divisions therein... 42:13. These Qur'anic texts preclude the notion of narrow partisanship that may lead to hatred or even violence against communities who perceive themselves as followers of other prophets.

On Universal Human Dignity: The Qur'an gives various reasons for why each human being must be honored on account of being human, irrespective of his or her chosen beliefs. Such honor is symbolized by the way the Qur'an describes Allah's creation of the human being in the best of moulds and commands the angels to bow down in respect to Adam. The Qur'an confirms God's revelation to previous prophets that ...if anyone slays a human being, unless it be [punishment] for murder, or for spreading mischief on earth, it shall be as though he had slain all humankind; whereas, if anyone saves a life, it shall be as though he had saved the lives of all humankind 5:32. Beyond sanctity of life, in the Qur'an we read: Indeed We [God] have conferred dignity on the children of Adam 17:70.

On Universal Human Brotherhood: Addressing the entire human race, the Qur'an states: O humankind! We [Allah] have created you from a single [pair] of a male and a female and have made you into nations and tribes, so that you may come to know one another. Verily, the most honored of you in the sight of Allah is the most righteous of you. Surely, Allah is all-knowing, all-aware 49:13. It must be noted that this verse does not address Muslims exclusively, but begins with the inclusive address —O humankind, an address that embraces all.

On Universal Peaceful Coexistence: The basic rule governing the relationship between Muslims and non-Muslims is that of peaceful co-existence, justice and compassion. The following two verses are key verses that embody that general rule: As for such [non-Muslims] who do not fight you on account of [your] faith, or drive you forth from your homelands, God does not forbid you to show them kindness [also love and respect] and to deal with them with equity, for God loves those who act equitably. God only forbids you to turn in friendship and alliance towards those who fight against you because of [your] faith, and drive you forth from your homelands or aid [others] in driving you forth.

On Peaceful Dialogue, Especially With The "People Of The Book": The Qur'an instructs Muslims: And do not argue with the People of the Book except in a most kindly manner, except for those of them who are bent on evil doing, and say: We believe in the revelation which has come down to us and in that which has come down to you; our Lord and yours is One and it is to Him that we [all] submit ourselves. [29:46] Not only do Muslims, Christians, and Jews share belief in the One God and divine revelation, they also share belief in human responsibility, consequences of good and evil deeds, moral teachings and other values such as love, peace and justice.

On Holy War Against Other Religions: It may be argued, from a religious perspective that the expression "Holy War" is a contradiction in terms, as there is nothing holy about war and its results: bloodshed, destruction and human suffering. Jihad is an

Arabic term derived from the root —J-H-D which means, literally, to strive or exert effort. The term Jihad and similar terms derived from the same root are used in the Qur'an and Hadeeth.

Firstly, it is used in the context of prayers, doing righteous deeds and self-purification; inward Jihad or struggle against evil inclinations within oneself [Qur'an, 22:77-78; 29:4-7].

Secondly, it is used in the context of social Jihad, or striving for truth, justice and goodness in one's relationship with other humans. Examples of this usage include the payment of charity to the needy [49:15] and striving to persuade those who reject God's message by referring to the arguments presented in the Qur'an [25:52]. Thirdly, it is used in the context of the battlefield, which is often called, more specifically, *qital*, which means 'fighting.' That latter form, the combative Jihad, is allowed in the Qur'an for legitimate self-defense in the face of unprovoked aggression or in resisting severe oppression on religious or other grounds.

On The Misinterpretation That The Qur'an Refers To Jews And Christians As Kuffar Or Infidels: In the English dictionary, an infidel is a person who has no religious faith. Does the Qur'an say that the Jews and Christians do not believe in Allah? No. Surah 29, verse 46, says that the God of Christians, Jews and Muslims is one and the same. The word infidel is an inaccurate translation of the word kafir in this case.

A Buddhist Perspective

Adrian Fish, a photo-based art teacher and novice priest in the Soto Zen school of Buddhism presents Buddhist ethical guidelines addressing the topic:
The Golden Rule: Do Unto Others As You Would Like Others Do Unto You.
The presentation was delivered at the Spiritual Diversity Conference, Halifax, Canada, October 2013

The Buddhist ethical guidelines, known as the ten precepts, are remarkably similar in content to the Ten Commandments, as they include the following admonitions:

1. Do not kill - affirm life 2. Do not take what is not given/respect things of others. 3. Do not misuse sexuality - cultivate honest relationships. 4. Do not lie/speak the truth. 5. Do not indulge in intoxicants - cultivate internal clarity. 6. Do not slander others - cultivate respectfulness. 7. Do not praise yourself at expense of others - abide in awakened nature. 8. Do not covet possessions - cultivate mutual support. 9. Do not harbour ill-will - practice loving kindness and understanding. 10. Do not abuse three treasures - support community that encourages awakening.

In spite of the similarities to the basic laws outlined in Judeo-Christianity, there is a difference in the spirit in which these are interpreted. In order to illuminate these differences, we must understand the fundamental difference in the Buddhist perspective as compared to those of monotheistic traditions. One such difference is the principle of *anatman* (no self).

This can be understood to mean that the self we believe to be a fixed, solid, substantial entity called 'I' is, in fact, illusory. This is not to say that there is not a relative self that lives in a relative world with relative rules and laws, but rather that this relative perspective is incomplete.

In Zen, we are tasked with grasping the complete truth directly, through our own experience in the practice of *zazen* or meditation. When addressing the topic of ourselves, we must pause to question whether the truth we think we refer to is complete, rather than just a relative, mutable, shifting truth. Through *zazen*, we begin to see the disintegration of our neat little moral categories. The emphasis on parsing right and wrong falls squarely on our shoulders.

My teacher, Zenkai Taiun Roshi, often states that we observe the precepts when we break them. We must note that it is, in fact, impossible not to break even the most basic precept of not killing, for example, virtually every moment we are alive. Our survival depends on transgressing this precept every moment, as any biologist would observe the incessant killing factory that is our body. Critical bodily functions such as digestion and disease immunity illustrate this point quite simply.

The precept of lying, for example, is implicit in virtually all the others. We can understand this from the conventional position of communication with malicious intent. We can also think of it as an act of omission as well as commission. When we introduce the concept of *anatman*- the principle of no substantial self, one can see that selfhood in the conventional sense is, in fact, a type of lie.

We must note that there is a critical need for navigating through our complex cultural world. Out of necessity, we must develop our personhood, or persona. The etymology of this word comes from the Latin *dramatis personae* or 'characters of the drama.' We define our self as a character in a performance of everyday life that is, if you will, a type of lie.

This latter type of lie is the most insidious of all given that it seeps its way into our consciousness without really seeming to be constructed at all. We can see a fundamental confusion between what we believe to be real or natural, versus what is, in fact, constructed or conventional. "Natural" typically refers to something that is derived from nature, so as to imply free from affectation. Convention can be defined as a culturally-specific norm - a perspective that fundamentally informs a specific world-view, typically without one's conscious awareness.

I discussed killing and lying, but an examination of some of the other precepts viewed through this lens may offer similar insights. In not taking what is not freely given, one could argue that the simple consumption of oxygen is a transgression of this precept. My teacher used the example of multiple people trapped in an airtight room. By definition, one's breathing takes away oxygen from another. Again, we must be clear that our conventional view of the world is not complete.

Misusing sexuality can be interpreted in many relative ways. Some Buddhist sects uphold abstinence, whereas others sanction marriage in non-monastic orders. But what does this precept really mean to you? Does it mean respecting the bond of trust developed between two partners? Does it define the gender of these two theoretical partners? Unlike other traditions, Buddhism is mute on these details.

The precept surrounding intoxicants has many interpretations. Some sects (such as those in the Hinayana school) observe this literally through the total abstention of alcohol. Other sects understand this more metaphorically, viewing it as the ways in which we intoxicate ourselves with false ideas and beliefs.

There are many good reasons to lie to ourselves, mostly having to do with bolstering the false notions about who we are. It's soothing to live in a fool's paradise, even when we know we're playing the part of the fool. Amazingly, we can play these dual roles, only admitting to it, to even ourselves in times of great strain or exhaustion. Clearly, we are complex creatures.

Coveting possessions is likewise read in some sects as renunciation, while others emphasize one's attitude towards possessions. It is possible to have many things but not hold an attitude of attachment that causes suffering, while at the same time, it is possible to own nothing but a robe and bowl and still be consumed by desire. Things are not always what they seem.

The practice of *zazen* allows us to cultivate the space to see the differences between relative and complete. The spillover effect of this practice helps us calibrate our internal moral compass, filling out the vague ethical generality of the precepts as written. The flexibility of interpretation obliges us to find out the true meaning of the non-transgression of the precepts for ourselves. The internalization of the precepts allows us to live in our awakened nature and actualize their essence: to do no harm, do good, and to do good for others.

A Bahá'í Perspective

Gordon Naylor, of the National Spiritual Assembly of the Bahá'ís of Canada speaks to conference delegates on *The Oneness Of Humanity*. These notes are only excerpts from his presentation to the Spiritual Diversity Conference, Halifax, Canada, October 2011.

In one of the panel discussions these last couple of days, a question raised was how do we create forums and opportunities for diverse religions and faiths to share with each other and why is that important for us to do as a society. Our interest should not be in justifying the value of our existence to a secular society, which is obviously how one is sometimes made to feel but rather how can all of these positive spiritual institutions work together with people of faith and of no faith to improve our civilization.

The purpose of religion is to bring people together. As we know, the meaning of the word 'religion' is 'that which binds'. Therefore, the intention of religion has always been to bring together various people in a state of unity of belief in God. To create a oneness. To unify people.

The Bahá'í sacred writings state that:

"Likewise, the divine religions of the holy Manifestations of God are in reality one though in name and nomenclature they differ. Man must be a lover of the light no matter from what day-spring it may appear. He must be a lover of the rose no matter in what soil it may be growing. He must be a seeker of the truth no matter from what source it come. Attachment to the lantern is not loving the light. Attachment to the earth is not befitting but enjoyment of the rose which develops from the soil is worthy. Devotion to the tree is profitless but partaking of the fruit is beneficial. Luscious fruits no

114

matter upon what tree they grow or where they may be found must be enjoyed. The word of truth no matter which tongue utters it must be sanctioned. Absolute verities no matter in what book they be recorded must be accepted. If we harbour prejudice it will be the cause of deprivation and ignorance. The strife between religions, nations and races arises from misunderstanding."

We are a religiously pluralistic society trying to function in a multiculturally secular dominant environment. Anyone can see why, as a community, we will have challenges. Things will have to change. We haven't considered deeply enough the real issue facing our country and the world in general. That issue concerns what happens when you strip religion and spirituality out of society. What you are left with as one writer put it, is a niche void. Where there is no belief systems or values that are identified and consciously committed to, then a society can fall victim to all manner of negative influences. Assisting individuals to determine their own moral compass in their search for meaning has always been the work of religion and faith.

There is a more substantial issue at stake when we do not recognize the value of religion and its role in civilization. The Universal House of Justice of the Bahá'í community in April 2000 stated:

There is a pressing challenge to be faced: Our children need to be nurtured spiritually to be integrated into the life of the Cause. They should not be left to drift in a world so laden with moral dangers. In the current state of society, children face a cruel fate. Millions and millions in country after country are dislocated socially. Children find themselves alienated by parents and other adults whether they live in conditions of wealth or poverty. This alienation has its roots in a selfishness that is born of materialism that is at the core of the godlessness seizing the hearts of people everywhere. The social dislocation of children in our time is a sure mark of a society in decline; this condition is not, however, confined to any race, class, nation or economic condition - it cuts across them all. Creating that change is the work of religious communities.

Religion must provide that moral compass and support to rehabilitate the fortunes of humankind. We must be the ones willing to make that difference in helping to educate and uplift the masses. Really this development always starts with a conversation. As we discuss issues, we have our own consciousness raised.

This raising of consciousness leads to development and action as a result. By faith communities working together or at least becoming aware of what each other is doing about important issues, more is accomplished to alleviate the suffering of humanity. By beginning to discuss ideas and thoughts we start a process to elevate the human condition. Let us distinguish ourselves by the deeds we carry out that make a difference in the world.

Canada, like the United Nations, is beginning to recognize that peace requires the involvement of peoples of all faiths. The Bahá'í International Community states that:

It is becoming increasingly clear that passage to the culminating stage in the millennia-long process of the organization of the planet as one home for the entire human family cannot be accomplished in a spiritual vacuum. Religion, the Bahá'í Scriptures aver, is the source of illumination, the cause of development and the animating impulse of all human advancement and has been the basis of all civilization and progress in the history of mankind. It is the source of meaning and hope for the vast majority of the planet's inhabitants, and it has a limitless power to inspire sacrifice, change and long-term commitment in its followers. It is, therefore, inconceivable that a peaceful and prosperous global society – a society which nourishes a spectacular diversity of cultures and nations – can be established and sustained without directly and substantively involving the world's great religions in its design and support.

This statement goes on to say:

At the same time, it cannot be denied that the power of religion has also been perverted to turn neighbour against neighbour. The Bahá'í Scriptures state that — religion must be the source of

116

fellowship, the cause of unity and the nearness of God to man. If it rouses hatred and strife, it is evident that absence of religion is preferable and an irreligious man is better than one who professes it.

To sum up, true religion has enriched the world with such a vast array of text that this source of knowledge must be regarded as one of the major ways of 'knowing' what the human race has for its illumination. This ocean of religious knowledge and the wisdom contained therein is impossible to ignore. Nor is it conceivable that the human race would deny its value to the civilizing processes of the world.

ACKNOWLEDGEMENTS

I abandoned the cause of this book several times since getting my teeth in it in the summer of 2017. Then on 8 July the following year, I forgot about it altogether when my wife, Teresa, was diagnosed with ovarian cancer and those dark clouds engulfed us all. The manuscript lay somewhere at the corner of my desk and stared at me occasionally as it collected dust, until New Year's Eve when my wife moved to remission.

This book, I thought, was important for someone who is struggling with those grave conundrums of life and is confused about the mysteries of the universe that continue to bewilder science to this day. On the other hand, while this book was intended to serve as a riposte to arguments that God is a delusional pre-occupation among the silly-headed, I also had to bring a new conversation to the table pointing to the fact that the search for the 'God mystery' cannot be pursued by an intellectual tool - such as science is - in worlds where fact and truth are established by empirical evidence alone. That pursuit would, forever, be futile because science would be looking for God in the wrong place.

So, I brushed off the dust from my manuscript in January this year with a sterling resolve to put this book in the hands of people who are looking for insights to those grave questions: How did I get here? Why am I here, anyway? Where am I going at the end of it all?

But I could not have done this without first speaking to Dr. Stephen Weppner, a scientist and a dear friend, who is also professor of Physics at Eckerd College in Florida. He and I spoke late into the night in the summer of July 2017 and in the morning, he told me over a cup of coffee, he would take this ride on the bus with me. "I am interested," he said. I am grateful to Stephen Weppner, whose foreword to the book is a solid buttress to the arguments I have laid out to defend its title.

I am grateful to family: My son, Aaron, who designed the cover and formatted the book and engaged with me on content, and his wife Kristina who patiently lent an ear to our conversations on this topic. I am grateful to Stephen, my son-in-law, who gleaned through the book twice, making subtle recommendations in editorial presentation after the first read and after the second run, nudged me and said: "It's ready to go."

I am grateful to two intelligent secularists with whom I put the book to test: first, my friend Don Kydd, who took up the book, gleaned through it and told me the book's narrative was without prejudice and therefore very readable; and second, to Marc Selles, my son-in-law, who began the read starting with Chapter 11. I cannot forget to thank Remy Taherbhoy, who first picked up the first raw draft and sat with me to discuss its contents.

I am in debt to my daughters, Golda, a journalist and news podcast specialist in New York, who gave the book a thorough read, made recommendations and flagged a green signal; and Esther, a communications specialist in London, who has promised to deploy her skills to put this book in the hands of people keen to lend an ear to conversations that unravel life's challenges.

I acknowledge with gratitude the many publishing houses, universities, newspaper and research organizations, who graciously granted me permissions to reprint quotes from their copyrighted material under the fair use provisions of the copyright law. I am indebted to the several conference speakers who have contributed their voice to the conversation from the perspective of interfaith dialogue which can be catalytic in shaping the *one-world, one humanity* dream.

Finally, I am grateful and immensely indebted to my dear and beloved wife Teresa, a science academic who discussed both scientific truths and science fiction with me and presented to me Dr. Francis Collin's book *The Language of God*, which prompted me to sidle up and join the conversation with my observations about the God who eludes science.

Without her support and patience, this book may never have rolled off the printing machines and fallen in the hands of the curious intellectual.

REFERENCES

Foreword

1. Schrödinger Erwin: My View of the World, Cambridge University Press, 1951, ISBN-9781107049710

Chapter 1

1. Darwin, Charles, *On the Origin of Species*, 1st edition, The Project Gutenberg eBook, Chapter 14: Recapitulation and Conclusion, 39th paragraph.
2. Diagoras <en.wikipedia.org/wiki/Diagoras_of_Melos>
3. Democritus <en.wikipedia.org/wiki/Democritus>
4. Epicurus <en.wikipedia.org/wiki/Epicurus>
5. Rationalism <en.wikipedia.org/wiki/Rationalism>
6. Center for the Study of Global Christianity, "*Christianity in its Global Context, 1970–2020: Society, Religion and Mission,*" report produced at Gordon-Conwell Theological Seminary, June 2013. Reprinted with permission.
7. Dawkins, Richard <en.wikipedia.org/wiki/Richard_Dawkins>
8. Albert Einstein: *The Human Side* (1979) *New Glimpses From His Archives* (1979), p.66 of the 1981 edition. Helen Dukas and Banesh Hoffmann. Princeton University Press. Reprinted with permission
9. Anthony de Mello, *Heart of the Enlightened*. Copyright© 1989 by the Center of Spiritual Exchange, DeMello Stroud Spirituality Center, ISBN 0 00 6274528. Reprinted with permission.

Chapter 2

1. en.wikipedia.org/wiki/Big_Bang

2. en.wikipedia.org/wiki/Steady_state_model. See also: Kragh, Helge (1999) *Cosmology and Controversy: The Historical Development of Two Theories of the Universe.* Princeton University Press, ISBN - 9780691005461

3. Collins, S. Francis, *The Language of God*, Free Press, A division of Simon & Schuster, Inc. ISBN: -13: 9781416542742, p.63-64. Reprinted with permission.

4. en.wikipedia.org/wiki/Discovery_of_cosmic_microwave_background_radiation Penzias, A.A.; R. W. Wilson (July 1965). "*A Measurement Of Excess Antenna Temperature At 4080 Mc/s*". Astrophysical Journal Letters.

5. Hoyle, Fred. *The Big Bang in Astronomy*, New Scientist, Vol. 92, No. 1280 (November 19, 1981), p. 527. Reprinted with permission.

6. Hoyle, Fred (November 1981). "*The Universe: Past and Present Reflections*", Engineering and Science, Volume 45:2, pp.12. Reprinted with permission.

7. helix.northwestern.edu/article/origin-life-panspermia-theory. Reprinted with permission.

8. NIH US National Library of Medicine: profiles.nlm.nih.gov/SC/Views/Exhibit/narrative/doublehelix.html

9. Anthony de Mello, *Prayer of the Frog*, Gujarat Sahitya Prakash, January 1, 2003 ISBN-13: 978-8187886259. Printed with permission.

Chapter 3

1. Paley, William, *Natural Theology: or, Evidences of the Existence and Attributes of the Deity, collected from the Appearances of Nature*, 1802. Vol. 1. Chapter 1: State of the Argument, p.1. Cited in: <en.wikipedia.org/wiki/Watchmaker_analogy>

2. Darwin, Charles, *(1859) On the Origin of Species by Means of Natural Selection, or the Preservation of Favoured Races in the Struggle for Life (1st ed). p.61*

3. Darwin, Charles, *On the Origin of Species*, The Project Gutenberg eBook, Chapter IV: Natural Selection or Survival of the Fittest - Summary of Chapter – 1st paragraph.

4. Darwin, Charles, *On the Origin of Species,* The Project Gutenberg eBook, Chapter VII: Instinct. 2nd paragraph.

5. Darwin, Charles, *On the Origin of Species*, The Project Gutenberg eBook, Chapter VI: Difficulties on Theory - Organs of Extreme Perfection and Complication – 1st paragraph.

6. Darwin, Charles, *On the Origin of Species*, The Project Gutenberg eBook, Chapter X1V: Recapitulation and Conclusion. 39th paragraph.

7. Darwin, Charles, *On the Origin of Species*, The Project Gutenberg eBook, Chapter XIV: Recapitulation and Conclusion. Final paragraph.

8. en.wikipedia.org/wiki/Religious_views_of_Charles_Darwin

9. Cornwell, John, *Darwin's Angel*, Profile Books, ISBN: 978-1-84668-048-9, p.129-130. Reprinted with permission.

Chapter 4

1. *Columbia* -Knights of Columbus, June 2017, p.13. Columbia@kofc.org. Reprinted with permission.

2. Saint Augustine, *The Literal Meaning of Genesis* I, Chapter XVIII, 37. Modern translation by J.H. Taylor (Newman Press, New York: 1982)

3. en.wikipedia.org/wiki/Yom

4. Bill Clinton's speech in the White House celebrating the completion of the first survey of the Entire Human Genome. Courtesy: National Human Genome Research Institute.

5. Einstein, Albert, *Science and Religion (1941) A Symposium, published by the Conference on Science, Philosophy and Religion in Their Relation to the*

Democratic Way of Life, New York (1941), Science and Religion, Section II, paragraph 4 < www.sacred-texts.com/aor/einstein/einsci.htm>

Chapter 5

1. *Scientific American* <www.scientificamerican.com/article/hawking-vs-god>
2. Broussard, Karlo,<strangenotions.com/does-science-make-god-irrelevant>
3. *Know This*, Edited by John Brockman, HarperCollins Publishers, ISBN 978-0-06-256206-7, p.93. Reprinted with permission.
4. Ibid, p.115-116
5. Oparin, Alexander, (1894-1980), *Important Scientists, The Physics of the Universe,* <www.physicsoftheuniverse.com/scientists_oparin.html>
6. Schroeder, L. Gerald, *The Hidden Face of God*, Simon & Schuster, p.58, ISBN-0-7432-0325-9. Reprinted with permission.
7. Hawking, Stephen, *A Brief History of Time*, Penguin Random House, p.133-135. ISBN- 9780553109535. Reprinted with permission,
8. Cornwell, John, *Darwin's Angel*, Profile Books Limited, p.64. ISBN-13:978-1-84668-048-9. Reprinted with permission
9. Anthony de Mello, *Prayer of the Frog*, Gujarat Sahitya Prakash, January 1, 2003, ISBN-13: 978-8187886259. Reprinted with permission.

Chapter 6

1. Vonnegut, Kurt, *A Man Without A Country*, Seven Stories Press p.66. ISBN 13:978-1-58322-713-8 Reprinted with permission.
2. Dawkins, Richard, *The God Delusion*, Houghton Mifflin Harcourt, ISBN-13: 978-0-618-91824-9. p.110. Reprinted with permission.
3. Cornwell, John, *Darwin's Angel*, Profile Books Limited, p.44, ISBN: 978-1-84668-048-9. Reprinted with permission.
4. plato.stanford.edu/archives/spr2019/entries/james/ Reprinted with permission.

5. en.wikipedia.org/wiki/Mysticism>

6. Ibid.

7. Ibid.

8. Merton, Thomas, *Seven Storey Mountain*, Houghton Mifflin Harcourt, 1998 p.123. ISBN 9780547543819. Reprinted with permission.

9. McHargue, Mike, *Finding God in the Waves*, Convergent Books, (Penguin Random House) p.128. ISBN: 978-1-101-90604-0. Reprinted with permission.

10. www.pewresearch.org/fact-tank/2016/06/01/10-facts-about-atheists/

11. Dawkins, Richard, *The God Delusion,* Houghton Mifflin Harcourt, p.125 ISBN-13: 978-0-618-91824-9. Reprinted with permission.

12. Anthony de Mello, *Prayer of the Frog*, Gujarat Sahitya Prakash, January 1, 2003, ISBN-13: 978-8187886259. Reprinted with permission.

Chapter 7

1. en.wikipedia.org/wiki/Edict_of_Milan

2. *2000 years of Christianity*, a special report of the *National Post*, p.8, Courtesy: Postmedia

3. Saint Augustine, *City of God*, Vol. II, Project Gutenberg eBook, 19:15, p.324

4. en.wikipedia.org/wiki/William_Wilberforce

5. Anscombe Elizabeth, <plato.stanford.edu/archives/spr2019/entries/anscombe> Reprinted with permission.

6. Mill, J. Stuart, *"Utilitarianism"* (1863), E-book: <www.utilitarianism.com/mill5.htm> Chapter 5, paragraph 12. Courtesy BLTC Research: <www.bltc.com>

7. Njoroge, M. John, *Must the Moral Law Have a Lawgiver*, Ravi Zakaria International Ministries. <www.rzim.org/read/just-thinking-magazine/must-the-moral-law-have-a-lawgiver> Reprinted with permission.

8. Ibid

9. McHargue, Mike, *Finding God in the Waves*, Convergent Books

(Penguin Random House), p.156, ISBN 978-1-101-90604-0.
Reprinted with permission.

10. Lewis, C.S., *Mere Christianity*, © copyright CS Lewis Pte Ltd 1942, 1943, 1944, 1952. Reprinted with permission.

11. Njoroge, M. John, *Must the Moral Law Have a Lawgiver,* Ravi Zacharias International Ministries, <rzim.org/just-thinking/must-the-moral law-have-a-lawgiver/> Reprinted with permission.

12. Lewis, C.S., *Mere Christianity*, © copyright CS Lewis Pte Ltd 1942, 1943, 1944, 1952. Reprinted with permission.   .

13. Njoroge, M. John, *Must the Moral Law Have a Lawgiver,* Ravi Zacharias International Ministries, <rzim.org/just-thinking/must-the-moral law-have-a-lawgiver/> Reprinted with permission.

14. Anthony de Mello, *Heart of the Enlightened.* Copyright©1989 by the Centre of Spiritual Exchange, ISBN 0 00 627452 8. DeMello Stroud Spirituality Center, NY, New York, Reprinted with permission.

Chapter 8

1. en.wikipedia.org/wiki/Black_Death

2. en.wikipedia.org/wiki/Spanish_flu

3. en.wikipedia.org/wiki/World_War_II_casualties

4. Darwin, Charles, *On the Origin of Species*, The Project Gutenberg eBook, Chapter III: Struggle for Existence, 11th paragraph.

5. Graham, Billy, ©2001 The Billy Graham Literary Trust. Reprinted with permission. All rights reserved.

6. Defoe, Daniel, *The Life and Adventures of Robinson Crusoe*, (1919) Project Gutenberg eBook, Chapter XV, paragraph 14

7. Extract from a presentation by Royal Pandit Bhikkhu Saranapala at the first Spiritual Diversity Conference hosted in 2011 in Halifax.

8. A presentation by Shastri Robert Gailey, Halifax Shambhala Centre, at the 2016 Spiritual Diversity Conference in Halifax.

9. Merton, Thomas-*The Seven Storey Mountain*, Houghton Mifflin Harcourt, 1998, p. 59-60, ISBN-9780547543819

10. Dr. Jonathan Sarfati, *Why Should a Loving God Allow Death and Suffering*, Creation Ministries International, <creation.com/why-death-suffering>. Reprinted with permission.

11. Ibid

Chapter 9

1. Vonnegut, Kurt, *Man without a Country,* Seven Stories Press, p.80-81, ISBN 13: 978-1-58322-713-8. Reprinted with permission.

2. *What Life Means to Einstein* article © SEPS. An Interview by George Sylvester Viereck, *The Saturday Evening Post*, Oct. 26, 1929, p. 17. Reprinted with permission.

3. en.wikipedia.org/wiki/List_of_apologies_made_by_Pope_John_Paul_II

4. *2000 years of Christianity*, a special report of the *National Post*, p.4 Courtesy: Postmedia. Reprinted with permission.

5. Hitchens, Christopher, *God is Not Great-Religion Poisons Everything*, Twelve Books (Hachette Group)

6. Rummel, R.J., *The Killing Machine in Marxism*, WorldNetDaily. <www.wnd.com/2004/12/28036/>

7. Zirkle, Conway, *Evolution, Marxian Biology and the Social Scene* (Philadelphia: University of Pennsylvania Press, 1959), pp.85-87. Cited in <www.icr.org/article/stalins-brutal-faith/>

8. Solzhenitsyn, Aleksandr, 1983 Templeton Address, *National Review*, December 11, 1983. 'Men Have Forgotten God'. Reprinted with permission.

9. Anthony de Mello, *The Heart of the Enlightened*. Copyright©1989 by the Centre of Spiritual Exchange, ISBN 0 00 627452 8. DeMello Stroud Spirituality Center, NY, New York. Reprinted with permission.

Chapter 10

1. *2000 years of Christianity*, a special report of the *National Post*, p.4. Courtesy: Postmedia. Reprinted with permission.
2. Ibid, p.41
3. Ibid, p.26
4. Ibid, p.42
5. Ibid, p. 54
6. Knights of Columbus, A Revolution of Conscience, <www.kofc.org/en/columbia/detail/revolution-of-conscience.html> Reprinted with permission.
7. Columbia, K of C, May 2017, p.9-p.10. Reprinted with permission.
8. en.wikipedia.org/wiki/Mother_Teresa
9. www.truah.org/wp-content/uploads/2018/12/TRUAH-2016-2017-Annual-Report.pdf Reprinted with permission.
10. www.thursdaysinblack.co.za
11. www.akdn.org/frequently-asked-questions

Chapter 11

1. Dr. Jonathan Sarfati, *Why Should a Loving God Allow Death and Suffering*, Creation Ministries International, <creation.com/why-death-suffering>. Reprinted with permission.
2. Darwin, Charles, *On the Origin of Species*, The Project Gutenberg eBook, Chapter III: Struggle for Existence, 11th paragraph.

www.ingramcontent.com/pod-product-compliance
Lightning Source LLC
LaVergne TN
LVHW011359080426
835511LV00005B/351